ALC

and other drugs

A practical guide to a positive response

George Ruston

Scripture Union
130 City Road, London EC1V 2NJ

Dedicated to Glenis, Simon, Rebecca, Bethan and my friends who gave me so much encouragement.

George Ruston is Executive Director of the UK Band of Hope, part of the youth leadership team at Bromley Baptist Church and a member of his local Family Health Service Authority.

First published 1991

British Library CIP Data
A catalogue record for this book is available from the British Library.

ISBN 0 86201 485 1

Acknowledgements

My thanks are due to the staff of Christian rehabilitation houses who helped me to understand their work, to the Churches Council on Alcohol and Drugs for allowing me to quote from the booklet *Alcohol On The Premises?*, and to Wendy Whitbread, for her patience whilst typing out the manuscript . . . again and again!!

The Twelve Traditions of Alcoholics Anonymous are reprinted on page 100/101 with the permission of Alcoholics Anonymous World Services, Inc. Permission to reprint the Twelve Traditions does not mean that AA has reviewed or approved the contents of this publication. AA is a program of recovery from alcoholism. Use of the Twelve Traditions in connection with programs and activities which are patterned after AA but which address other problems does not imply otherwise.

Cover design by Sharyn Troughton

Phototypeset by Intype, London
Printed by Cox and Wyman Ltd, Reading, Berkshire

Contents

Foreword

Problems related to the use of alcohol and other drugs can often seem to be problems that affect other people – such as media stars who feature in gossip columns, young people smoking cannabis or 'down and outs' seen sleeping rough. But the media image reflects only the tip of a huge iceberg! In towns and villages up and down the country, near your home and mine, people are suffering due to their use of drugs.

What is worse, thousands of families and individuals are affected by other people's use of drugs – be it drunk drivers, accidents caused by lunch-time drinking or violence in the home. People we know – especially the young – are at risk. And it's not just illegal drugs like heroin, cocaine and cannabis that are the problem. How many people realise that most of the harm related to drug abuse is linked with alcohol and tobacco?

Can we, as Christians, make some response to this situation? Yes, we can! We may not solve all the world's problems, but with God's help we can make a difference. And that's why I'm pleased to see this book, because it's not primarily about bad news – it's about the good news that everyone can be part of a growing 'movement for change'.

Here's to healthy, happy, drug-free living!

Cheers!

Roy Castle

1

What's the problem?

'I began sniffing at 15 when everyone else seemed to be doing it. I wanted the "high" it gave as well as the attention. It wasn't always good. It frightened me at times, but this didn't make any difference. It had reached a really bad stage when school teachers noticed and told my parents. They tried to get help and this made a difference for a while. Stopping made me bad-tempered, edgy and depressed and so I sniffed again – even at home.

'I had fits and hallucinated, frightening myself as well as others: stories about me "frothing at the mouth" were being passed around. Eventually I wanted a longer-lasting experience and moved on to other drugs. My life was a mess and I needed help. I had to stop and did so at last because I became a Christian. My faith gave me something stronger than my habit.'

Christians will recognise this as a classic 'drugs testimony'. Faith in Jesus *has* saved all kinds of people from themselves and their problems. Drug addicts *can* find salvation in Christ – but for most it will not come quickly. For many it will never happen. Instant solutions are the exception rather than the rule, and Christians who work with addicts will confirm this sad fact. It takes a great deal of time, love and commitment to help because addiction enslaves body and mind.

Exploding myths

There is a mythology which has grown up around the drug issue. Question any group of ordinary people – Christians included – about drugs and it is likely that popular myth will prevail over reality. For example, the widely-held belief that heroin is the drug which most threatens our society is just not true. The drug which is in fact most used and causes the most harm is alcohol. It is legally and socially acceptable and the risks involved in its consumption are largely ignored. Yet this is a depressant drug which in Britain alone causes damage costing more than two billion pounds each year. The additional and incalculable costs of human suffering make alcohol abuse the hidden epidemic of our time.

Another myth is that drug problems are a disease of the young. Young people *are* more at risk because they are not physically or emotionally mature, but there is no magical cut-off point at the age of twenty! Older people have drug-related problems too. Elderly people may suffer from a mixture of prescribed medicines with what seems like a reasonable alcohol intake. Mixing drugs complicates matters and increases their effects disproportionately.

The 'myth of addiction' runs through all popular ideas about drugs. Many think that 'only addicts have drug problems'. Yet addiction is only the tip of an iceberg. 'Drug-related' problems cover a much wider range of social and health issues. Crime, road accidents, unwanted pregnancies, minor and major health conditions are related to the use of drugs long before addiction sets in – if it ever does.

The truth about drugs is not only stranger than fiction but much worse. We need to judge for ourselves using Christian principles and then consider our responses. It is impossible to classify drugs as solely a 'secular', 'educational', 'social', 'health' or any other sort of problem. We live in a drug-using society where the effects reach everywhere.

Into action

Although the subject of drug abuse is complicated, history has shown that the responses of ordinary people can play a large part in reducing human suffering. All of us have the ability to help solve the 'drugs problem' – but should Christians need to do anything about drug abuse? After all, there appears to be very little of it within churches! How many drug addicts does the average Christian know?

Despite some honourable exceptions, Christians today are not in the forefront of attempts to care for those suffering from drug abuse or prevent it happening in the first place. Things were different in the nineteenth century. Alcohol education was given social *and* spiritual dimensions as part of the Christian-led social reform movement. Christians cared for others by personal example and action. Midweek clubs run by the Band of Hope kept children away from drink – and drunken parents – and a Christian lifestyle was actively promoted. Hundreds of books and leaflets were written on the subject and 'Temperance Sunday' became a fixture for many churches. The effect on the public at large was a reduction in alcohol-related problems. The church led by example and Christians were 'up front'.

This century shows a different picture. Although smoking has decreased in the face of the evidence of health risks and the work of pressure groups such as Action on Smoking and Health (ASH), the use of other chemical substances has increased at dramatic rates. The consumption of alcoholic drinks, fuelled by a relative fall in price (allowing for inflation), has almost doubled since the 1950s. The traffic in illegal drugs has become big business with large profits to be made. Even the continuing anti-smoking publicity did not stop a mid-1980s rise in teenage smoking.

Although it is important to guard against oversimplification, Christians should ask themselves if all this would have happened if the church had shown as much social commitment as in the nineteenth century. The Royal College of Psychiatrists published a report (*Alcohol: Our Favourite Drug*) which suggested that successful anti-drug movements have had a religious rather than a secular grounding. Solutions to social problems need a moral/ethical dimension.

Christians working for nineteenth-century social reform saw that people were hurting and needed faith in Jesus. Taking their example from him they met these physical and spiritual needs. 'Social work' was a direct outworking of their faith in action. People became Christians partly because they saw Christ's message of salvation put into practice.

In this century major divisions arose between those who emphasised evangelism and others who were strong on social action. But consider Jesus' ministry: he combined social action with the good news of salvation and cared for people as well as encouraging them to become his disciples. Jesus was doctor, social worker, teacher, preacher and much more besides! He did tell his followers to 'Go and make disciples of all nations, baptising them in the name of the Father and of the Son and of the Holy Spirit' (Matthew 28: 19). But he continued, '. . . and teaching them to obey everything I have commanded you . . .'

Given Jesus' concern for the whole of life, it is not surprising that those times when the church has been strongest have been when evangelism was linked with a practical care for physical and social needs. The nineteenth-century Band of Hope movement clearly showed this as it exploded from nothing in 1847 to have over three million children and adults in membership at the turn of the century. Many of its workers aimed 'To win the young for Christ and total abstinence'. Evangelism, together with a concern about alcohol problems, added thousands to the church.

Christian social concern is again becoming a force to be reckoned with, although there is a real danger that 'drugs' will be left behind. When the Government announced its intention in 1987 to legislate for the afternoon opening of public houses there was no group which could easily take a leading interest, although some Christians were concerned. There was no focus for concern. The result was little effective opposition to a new Licensing Act which sped through Parliament in 1988.

There are very few Christian groups which specialise in the rehabilitation or counselling of addicts on illicit drugs. There are even fewer for the much larger number of alcoholics. This state of affairs led to the setting up of the Evangelical Coalition on Drugs which aims to convince the church at large that there is a problem within the community: a problem which Christians *can* do something about.

There are signs that the church today is beginning – at last – to wake up to the drugs issue. The Evangelical Alliance members who set up the Evangelical Coalition on Drugs are not the only Christians who see a need to respond to alcohol and other drug problems. Across all denominations and other Christian groups there has been a slow movement of individuals wanting to know more and caring enough to do something.

Generally, they are parents and workers who actually see young people at risk. They are still a minority, but their concern, which was hardly evident a few years ago, is an indication of the potential the church has to make a contribution to tackling the drugs problem. The following chapters will show how this can be achieved.

2

Face the facts!

The term 'drug' is often abused! A drug is technically a substance which alters the functioning of the body's metabolism. Drugs have positive uses. Medicine, for instance, relies heavily on the use of drugs to control pain and cure disease. This book is about those drugs which are 'socially used or abused' – or, in other words, consumed in a non-medical context.

Some drugs are used socially without causing trouble. Caffeine, for example, is a drug which millions of people drink on a daily basis in their tea, coffee or hot chocolate. Many will suffer no ill-effects from a small consumption of alcohol. Yet both caffeine and alcohol *can* cause ill-health and, in the case of alcohol, many more problems besides. For the purpose of this book it is sufficient to define drug abuse as something that adversely affects the human body – either mentally or physically. But how big a problem is drug abuse? And which drugs are most dangerous?

Drug abuse is, in general, on the increase. For example, the quest for sporting achievement has led to dramatic developments in drug testing to try to curb the temptations for athletes to cheat. Drugs can be used to speed up reaction time – valuable for tennis players. Drugs can be used for steadying the arm – beta blockers have brought controversy to snooker. And drugs can be used for developing body weight and strength in athletes. Ben Johnson, a Canadian sprinter, was stripped of his gold medal at the 1988 Olympics when tests revealed traces of an anabolic steroid after his 100 metres victory.

Our cultural background will also affect what we consider to be abuse. A West Indian, for example, may view cannabis as safe in most circumstances and feel that it is less harmful than alcohol or tobacco. Because, however, it is illegal to possess cannabis in Britain, many others feel that it must be highly dangerous. (The truth is that cannabis is less harmful than alcohol or tobacco.)

Periodically there are sensational news articles about solvent abuse – particularly when someone young has died. We might be forgiven for jumping to the conclusion that this is the most dangerous type of 'drug taking' for teenagers. In fact in 1990 there were only just over 100 deaths in Britain which were connected with solvents; solvent abuse is not the widespread killer that it is often thought to be.

Even more press coverage has been given to heroin. Undoubtedly the heroin trade is big (and illegal) business and brings with it human disaster on an increasing scale, but in 1985 there were eighty-two deaths attributed to all opiates (including heroin) and other illegal drugs. The popular myth which sees heroin as the biggest killer drug is simply not true. The report *Alcohol: Our Favourite Drug*, from the Royal College of Psychiatrists, goes on to make the point that there could be 25,000 deaths associated with alcohol each year. Even this is a low estimate compared to that given by the Royal College of General Practitioners, which suggests up to 40,000 deaths per year. Alcohol and tobacco emerge as much greater threats to personal health and the fabric of society than do all the illegal drugs put together.

Alcohol and other drug abuse is an issue which is surrounded with misinformation, half-truths and sensationalised stories. And so we need to start with a look at the various substances involved, what they are and what they do. It is impossible in a short book to cover all kinds of drugs which are abused on any scale, but the most significant (in terms of numbers of users) are described in this chapter.

Alcohol

Alcohol is perhaps the most misunderstood drug of them all. Many people do not even think of it as a depressant, addictive drug and relatively few understand its true nature. Using alcohol in drinks involves a risk – yet few people stop to make a sober assessment of the potential costs and benefits.

Chemistry students know that there are many different alcohols which form a 'series' of related substances. Methanol is the first in the series, and methylated spirits is a mixture of this and ethanol (the next in the series) with a chemical agent added to make it unpleasant to drink. Ethanol, sometimes called ethyl alcohol, is the type of alcohol found in alcoholic drinks. We will just call it alcohol for the sake of simplicity.

Pure alcohol is a colourless liquid with a burning taste. It looks like water but is a poison. It freezes at a lower temperature than water and this, coupled with its value as a solvent, gives it some valuable commercial uses. It is used in the preparation of perfumes and other toiletries, shoe polish, window cleaning creams, skin rubs for athletes and de-icing sprays for car windows. All these materials contain harmful substances and are extremely dangerous if they are consumed. Alcohol is sometimes used in medicines – some proprietary cough and cold mixtures contain it as do most brands of gripe water. (This means that people who cannot consume alcohol for health reasons or because of a history of alcoholism have to make sure they read the small print.)

Alcohol production

Alcohol is produced by mixing sugar, water and yeast. The yeast sets off the reaction which turns the sugary water into alcohol. In nature, grapes often have a whitish 'bloom' on the outside and this is the yeast substance which causes the sugar and water inside the grapes to ferment. The same process of fermentation occurred when the ancient Britons made mead by putting honey in water and left it out for airborne microscopic particles of yeast to float along on the breeze and set the reaction going.

Beer is made from cereal grain by a process of brewing and fermentation. The grain is crushed and soaked in water to produce malt, which is often flavoured with dried hops. Yeast is added for the fermentation process. It is impossible to obtain more that 14% alcohol by this method (because too much alcohol poisons the yeast!).

Drinks which have a high alcohol content, such as spirits and liqueurs, are produced by distillation. In very simple terms, the liquid is heated, and as alcohol boils at a lower temperature than water it is possible to collect an alcohol-rich 'steam' from the hot liquid. This is collected and cooled to produce a stronger drink.

Alcohol content

Alcoholic drinks vary enormously in type, taste and strength. Shandy is a mixture of beer and lemonade and can have a low alcohol content. At the other end of the scale, liqueurs contain up to 60% alcohol by volume. Beers, lagers and cider generally contain 4–9%; wines between 9–20%; and spirits such as gin, whisky and brandy up to 40%.

These percentages can be confusing. Whisky, for example, has a higher alcohol content than beer but is drunk in smaller quantities. So half a pint of strong beer will contain more alcohol than a single whisky.

The strength of drinks can be compared by using a

'unit of alcohol' as a standard measure. For example, a half pint of beer, a glass of wine and a single whisky all contain one standard unit. That means that two pints of beer will affect someone more than two single whiskies.

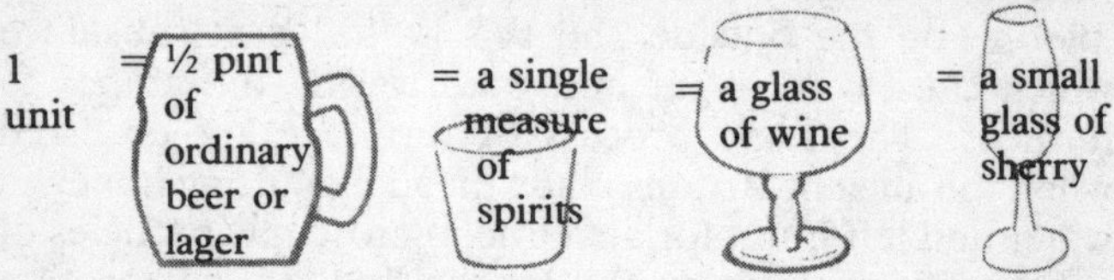

Of course this comparison can only be used as a rough guide – extra strength beers, ciders and lagers may be up to three times stronger than ordinary beers. And at home a genial dinner host will probably fill his guests' glasses and give them more than the 'standard' measure.

Alcohol in the body

Once consumed, alcohol leaves the human body at a standard rate. An average person removes alcohol at the rate of one unit per hour. This means that a dinner guest drinking three normal glasses of wine will have three hours to wait until his body is alcohol-free.

Exercise, sweating or black coffee will not speed up this process. Only between 6% and 10% of alcohol leaves the body through urine, breath or perspiration. The rest is 'oxidised' by the liver and it takes time to do this. This oxidisation process slowly damages the liver. A heavy drinker's liver will look more like a dried up portion of fried pig's liver than the healthy deep red/brown colour of the same liver when purchased.

While the oxidisation process is going on, alcohol will have entered the bloodstream and will reach all parts of the body. The brain will be affected, its higher level faculties being depressed. Judgment, self-control and reaction time are all impaired by small amounts of alcohol and the effect increases in proportion to the amount consumed. Alcohol helps people relax because it actually hits those brain functions which relate to shyness and caution. There is a lot of truth in the old saying that a person's real character comes out when they have been drinking!

The first effects of alcohol make a drinker feel pleasantly relaxed and he may soon become convinced he is the life and soul of the party. In reality, however, his brain has less control over what he says and so the standard of jokes and behaviour will fall rather than rise. Later on he may become aggressive and increasingly erratic. For others, the removal of inhibitions can mean they become weepy or depressed.

Alcohol complicates matters by affecting each one of us differently. Women are more susceptible than men because of their physiological make up – they weigh less and their livers are less able to cope with alcohol. Young people are even more vulnerable.

Medical studies have shown that 80% of cirrhosis of the liver, 10% of high blood pressure, strokes and heart disease, 10% of breast cancer and cancer of the mouth and 3% of all cancers are directly caused by heavy drinking. It also causes inflammation of the pancreas which can affect the body's ability to absorb nutrients and so lead to malnutrition and diabetes.

Heavy drinking can cause menstrual problems in women and can lead to a lack of interest in sex as well as infertility in both men and women. Pregnant women are advised not to drink because of the harmful effects alcohol can have on the foetus – like reduced birth weights and retarded development.

Excessive alcohol intake can cause depression, an inability to concentrate and even suicidal tendencies. These problems occur partly because alcohol is a depressant but also because it destroys brain cells – doctors have discovered that alcoholics' brains actually shrink in size. The average man runs a serious risk of long-term health problems if he drinks more than 21 units a week (10.5 pints of 'standard' beer). Women are at serious risk with a consumption of 14 units a week or more. Remember, though, that there are many other problems which relate to much lower levels of consumption.

Drinkers will find it harder to diet because, although alcohol is high in calories (there are 80 in a glass of wine and 150 or more in a pint of beer!), it does not provide any useful nutrients. Drinking helps increase body fat and regular beer drinkers often develop a 'pot belly'. Heavy drinkers can actually suffer from malnutrition, even though they may be overweight.

Social risks

One in five of the people who die on the roads are killed in accidents linked with alcohol consumption – either their own or someone else's. There were nearly 17,000 casualties in 1988 involved in incidents where at least one driver failed a breath test. Many of those casualties were not drinkers. In 1986 there were 101,000 convictions for drinking and driving, and many more get away with being over the limit. A significant proportion of those involved are not problem drinkers. Statistics are not collected for those situations where people may have consumed alcohol but are below the limit.

The Drew Report in 1962 said that 'alcohol is a primary and continuous depressant and in this respect it shows the characteristic action of general anaesthetics.' Drivers will feel they perform better after a few drinks but, in fact, the increase in reaction time and reduction in self-control makes them a menace on the roads. Even one unit of alcohol will have some effect. Someone who has drunk five units is, on average, four times more likely to have an accident than someone who has drunk two units. Five units is only two and a half pints of beer or five glasses of wine. Ten units will make the average person twenty-five times more likely to have an accident. Some people will be likely to have an accident at low levels of consumption because they are more susceptible to alcohol.

Paul Channon, Secretary of State for Transport in 1987, summed it up when he said, 'Just one small drink can make the difference between life and death.' But alcohol related social problems do not only loom on the roads: there are problems in families. This book could be filled with statistical evidence of the harm which alcohol can do. Alcoholics Anonymous produced a survey which showed that drink had played a significant part in 30% of divorces, and a study of 100 battered wives showed that just over half of their partners engaged in frequent heavy drinking. Much crime is alcohol related – up to 50% of burglaries are committed under the influence of alcohol. Accidents in the home or at work often owe their origins to alcohol. A report in 1977 from the Department of Trade and Industry linked alcohol consumption to 43% of deaths from falls and 39% of deaths from fires.

Then there is the financial cost – the British spend £50 million **a day** on alcohol: over 50% more than that spent on food. But there is a hidden cost, too – of over £2 **billion** annually in Britain. This includes the measurable costs of road accident damage, health care, industrial and criminal incidents. It does not begin to measure the intangible costs of human suffering and other stresses.

While figures do not exist for the amount of drink-induced vandalism, football hooliganism or rural 'lager-loutism', the Government took the link between drink and football seriously enough to legislate against the provision of alcohol within grounds and whilst fans are in transit. The 1990 World Cup saw Italian cities go 'dry' in an attempt to reduce the risk of riotous behaviour. The problem, however, is not just with excessive drinkers, but is for ordinary people.

Thomas Bewley, the President of the Royal College of Psychiatrists, has commented that '. . . although excessive drinkers will reduce their personal risk if they curtail their consumption, their numbers are so small that they will have little impact on the public health problem because most casualties are generated by the numerically much larger "lower risk" consumers in the community.' It is essential to grasp this because it is at the heart of the alcohol 'problem'. Alcohol abuse is not limited to those unfortunate souls who reside on 'Skid Row'. The person with an alcohol problem tomorrow could be in the church pew today. He or she might be alongside us at work, college, school or training scheme. And their problems begin now – as 'moderate' drinkers.

Benefits

Drink is part of the fabric of our society and a great many people will use it without coming to harm. They will enjoy the taste and appreciate the mild feeling of relaxation which one drink will bring. The place which wine has in the church is discussed more fully elsewhere in this book as many churches afford it an important place in the sacrament of communion and as a means of celebration. Taxes bring over £7 billion annually to the Government and the industry is an extremely large employer. Drink also figures heavily in our export trade and is worth over £1 billion annually to Britain's balance of payments.

Tobacco

Since Sir Walter Raleigh brought tobacco back from the Americas in the sixteenth century there has been a rise and fall in its popularity. From around 1960 there has been a massive shift in public opinion. This change in attitude has been accompanied by a reduction in overall consumption and a dramatic rise in the number of non-smokers. Although taxation has helped control consumption, the change has come about largely by education, pressure group politics and, most importantly, personal example.

Tobacco products release three dangerous substances which cause ill-health and 100,000 premature deaths in Britain each year. The first is carbon monoxide – a gas which readily combines with the haemoglobin in red blood cells. This reduces the blood's ability to carry oxygen by 10% or more for regular smokers. Poor muscle action and hardening of the arteries may lead to high blood pressure, strokes or heart attacks.

The second substance is tar – this can cause changes in the lung cells and promote the development of cancer. The incidence of lung cancer in smokers is much higher than in non-smokers and, despite modern methods of treatment, is a major cause of death. The third substance is nicotine – a habit forming stimulant drug. Smokers may say that cigarettes keep them calm, but their habit in fact creates tense feelings which start as the nicotine level in the blood drops and makes them want another cigarette. As the blood nicotine level rises again, relief is felt. Nicotine is a poison which narrows the blood vessels, speeds up the heart rate and raises blood pressure.

Although estimates vary, heavy smokers will, on average, lose as much as fifteen years of their life. Out of every 1,000 young people who smoke twenty cigarettes a day, six will be killed on the roads but 250 will end up prematurely dead because of their smoking. These deaths will be preceded by poorer health and a lower quality of life than that enjoyed by non-smokers. Pregnant women who smoke will pass the harmful substances to the foetus – resulting in lower birthweights and retarded development.

A smoker only inhales 25% of cigarette smoke, releasing the rest into the atmosphere. 'Passive smoking' describes the involuntary inhalation of smoke by non-smokers in the company of smokers. Medical research has demonstrated that this holds significant risks.

Non-smokers find it difficult to understand the hold that smoking exerts over others, especially young people. These comments from a teenager give a glimpse of life on the other side.

'I started smoking when I was ten years old – but it was just an on and off situation until I was thirteen when I started to smoke regularly. To get my cigarettes I nicked money or fags from my family. I suppose I started smoking just because I was hanging around with other people who smoked and I didn't want to be different. In fact all of my friends smoked and I thought that anyone who didn't smoke was odd and very stupid. People looked better when they smoked – harder. And I hate to admit it now, but I thought it made me look more grown up as well.

'When I see young kids smoking now, they look so daft and I realise that I probably looked the same. Shame!

'I knew people who said that smoking was bad for me but I just never thought I would become addicted. Yet I did try to give up at times, although I'm not sure why. I could never do it, especially when I was with people who smoked all the time. I honestly thought I would never be able to stop but now I've been spending more time with people who don't smoke and that has made me see things differently.

'I'm beginning to smoke a lot less and I now think it will be possible for me to give up for good.

'Although I feel the desire to smoke very strongly still – more to have something in my hand and to go through the motions of taking a drag, rather than because of the feeling it gives inside – I just try to keep myself busy. Anyway, I'm more aware of how disgusting it is to those who don't smoke. I can't get over how much it smells, and people's breath is so foul! I don't go on about their smoking – that's up to them – as long as they don't talk into my face while they do it! My advice to anyone has got to be DON'T SMOKE. If you don't start you won't have to try and give it up, will you?'

Solvent abuse

Solvent abuse is not illegal. In fact the only legal action which can be taken relates to suppliers. Shopkeepers can be prosecuted for selling products to young people if it can be proved they were going to be used for intoxication by means of inhalation. Not surprisingly, this has not led to many prosecutions!

Originally glues were the substances most used, hence the term 'glue-sniffing'. But many other volatile substances – not all of them solvents – are used, giving rise to the acceptance of the term 'solvent abuse' as a description. Glues are sniffed by perhaps 30% of users, although aerosols, butane gas, petrol and other volatile substances – often found in homes for domestic purposes – are also used. Fashion, effect and availability are the major factors which determine which are most popular.

A variety of surveys have shown that 6–9% of secondary school students have tried sniffing solvents and that it is more popular among boys than girls. An analysis of deaths between 1971 and 1985 showed the ratio of girls to boys as 1:10, but in 1986 this had changed to almost 1:5. Most people who sniff are between twelve and seventeen years old.

Solvent abuse can result in death, but usually as a result of the environment rather than the substance involved. 'Sniffing' is an activity often done in hiding, and surroundings like derelict land pose dangers to anyone, especially when 'under the influence'.

Of the ninety-two deaths in 1986, thirty-four were associated with the abuse of butane gas refills; twenty-one to aerosols; nineteen to typewriter correcting fluids, spot removers and other substances; and eighteen to solvents in glues. The average home probably contains thirty products which can be sniffed. Nearly half of those who died between 1971 and 1985 did so in their own home or that of a friend. Trends in sniffing do change – between 1971 and 1980 lighter fuel accounted for 26% of deaths. By 1989 it had risen to 50%. Sniffing glues is falling out of fashion.

Solvent abuse may damage blood cells, the heart and the nervous system. The harm done to the lungs can be lasting. Not only can the fumes make it more difficult to breathe, but they may permanently damage the lining of the air passages. When the fumes or substances come into contact with lips, mouth or nose they may burn the skin. It is quite common to see skin burns and sores around the noses and lips of sniffers. Solvents also irritate the lining of the stomach. This may lead to loss of appetite and then loss of weight. (See Appendix 3 for emergency action in cases of solvent abuse.)

Solvents quickly affect the brain because they are absorbed into the bloodstream in the same way as nicotine from tobacco smoke. Different substances do vary in their effect, but all work to produce a ‘buzz’. A ‘buzz’ is a giddy and light-headed feeling, similar to the first stages of being drunk. This often goes as quickly as it comes which encourages further attempts to bring back the feeling. Users may feel relaxed and at ease – ready to face anything the world is going to throw at them – because their brains have been affected. A ‘buzz’ may last from five up to forty minutes. A second stage, perhaps lasting for about an hour, finds the user sleepy, feeling sick or even unconscious. There may also be a loss of memory.

Not all who experiment with solvents become addicted and for most it never goes beyond the experimental stage. Lonely children with family problems are more likely to develop into regular users, but everyone who experiments is at risk. When users begin relying on a ‘buzz’ to see them through the day they will become an easier target for people selling illegal drugs. Sniffing can become a training ground for other drug abuse.

Cannabis

Cannabis comes from a plant and the drug is used as a relaxant and mild intoxicant. 'Hashish' or 'hash', the commonest form of cannabis in Britain, is resin scraped from the plant and compressed into blocks. Herbal cannabis, known in the USA as marihuana, is a preparation of the dried plant material.

In Britain cannabis is generally smoked, often with tobacco. Smoking allows the drug to enter the bloodstream very quickly and therefore the user can regulate the dose for desired effect. The possession or use of cannabis is illegal.

Some researchers have estimated that one in twenty of the British population have tried cannabis. Its effects depend largely on the user's mood and expectations. Most people do not experience very much at first. There is no conclusive evidence that long-term use causes lasting damage. This may be because there has been insufficient time to complete the type of study required to detect slow-to-develop and infrequent health problems. However cannabis smoke may cause bronchitis, respiratory disorders and lung cancer – just like tobacco smoke.

Cannabis does not seem to produce physical addiction, although users may feel mentally dependent upon its effect. Like any drug habit, it will make it easier for users to try other drugs.

Pete Townsend, guitarist for 'The Who', has said, 'I once attributed all my natural gifts to cannabis; my ability to play the guitar and to enjoy good music. So when I finally stopped using cannabis in 1967, after four years' use, I was very angry to discover than life could be just as good without it.'

Cannabis is less harmful than alcohol, although campaigners for legalisation tend to ignore the fact that it can still cause harm. This story shows the ill-effects one user experienced.

'I always thought that I would never become involved

in drug-taking of any kind. I didn't count alcohol in that – I thought it wasn't dangerous enough. I know better now!

'It didn't take me long, though, to decide to use cannabis (dope). Most of my friends were involved and they seemed to be OK – no shakes, bad experiences, etc. I started off refusing the 'joints' passed round but, because I was always with my friends when they smoked dope, I soon felt left out. So I tried it.

'Nothing really happened, and I was quite disappointed, wondering why people were laughing when I just felt tired. I thought they were pretending. I carried on smoking dope though and soon I found that I was joining in with the jokes and I was experiencing the paranoid feelings just like everyone else!

'I remember once when I had to get up and speak in front of people: I made certain that I had a smoke first – so that I could cope!

'I was introduced to the idea of inhaling, rather than smoking dope with tobacco, and this seemed to have a greater effect. It was also a lot easier than fumbling with cigarettes, papers, etc, to roll a 'joint'. On one occasion I went to friends for a meal and all but one of us got very high. I can remember laughing a lot until suddenly it all went wrong.

'People began to change, things were moving towards me, then going away and objects became really weird! I curled up on the bed, petrified. I felt as if my head was going to shake itself off! I sucked my thumb for comfort and then thought that I should stop because my teeth were biting through it. I vomited and tears were running down my face. I wanted to sit down and howl like a wolf. I shouted for help and held on to the one person who hadn't been involved. (She'd had a friend who had committed suicide whilst high on dope, so she wouldn't touch the stuff.) I needed her "normality". I could understand her friend though, because I knew that if I had been alone I would have ended my life – it was so horrible. She even had to stop me running in front of cars! I wanted a doctor and pleaded for them to get one, but they convinced me that I couldn't see one because we were involved in something illegal.

'Eventually the feeling went and I lay down, exhausted, and cried myself to sleep. I never want to feel that again – nothing would be worth it, so I stopped using cannabis. Luckily my friends understood and didn't hassle me.

'It was a while later that I discovered this sort of thing can happen to some cannabis users – only I hadn't known.

'I will never forget the fear that I felt!'

Cannabis illustrates the problems of determining which drugs should be legally available. It may be less harmful than alcohol or tobacco, but legalising it would only provide more opportunity for increasing the harm to which it is related.

Heroin

Heroin is not a new substance. Opiate drugs are derived from opium, the sap of the white or purple poppy. Opium has been valued for its ability to relieve pain: and it has been feared because of its addictive and destructive powers. Doctors have long tried to separate the two sides of opium, trying to keep the pain relieving property and yet avoid the risks. Morphine and heroin were developed as a result of these efforts. They have increased the ability to relieve pain but at the cost of a corresponding increase in addictive power.

As a person becomes addicted to heroin, more will be needed to produce the same 'high' and it will be needed more frequently in order to escape the pain of withdrawal. (This is called 'tolerance' and applies to other drugs as well.) This is true however the drug is used. Smoking heroin may be less dangerous than injection but the risks are considerable. It is more dangerous to inject as the drug then reaches the bloodstream in a more concentrated form. Impurities in the drug also go straight into the body. There are the additional infection hazards of using dirty needles and HIV/AIDS can result from sharing needles. Despite the common stereotype, however, most heroin users do not inject.

The effects of heroin are overplayed by the media, but it is still a very dangerous drug. People usually turn to it after using other drugs and may continue to be under the influence of more than one substance – like this young man.

'I am twenty-one and have just spent the last couple of months in a treatment centre for heroin addiction and alcoholism. It is impossible to fully explain the moral degradation of my addiction in a few words, but starting with my first smoke of hash my life was taken over – within eight months I was taking heroin every day.

'I come from a strong and loving family and the first eighteen years of my life were spent at good schools and in a secure, happy and drug-free environment. When I began using heroin my life had already been won over by drugs, they were my god and I would do nothing without them. I first used heroin to make me feel good, then to improve an evening out, and finally, in order to get out of bed and face the day so I could get some more.

'I have spent lots of money but my real loss is the emotional despair I inflicted on myself and those closest to me. It is these people who I have harmed the most. In some cases it is best that I never see them again, for to see me would perhaps do more harm than good – whatever my condition.

'Before I entered treatment my family had chosen, through love, to abandon me. One can only be exposed to a cold, emotionless machine, hell-bent on self-destruction, for so long. My addiction destroyed the bonds within the family. I did not care whether I lived or died, I was easy either way. In the end I was hated by all and I hated myself. My "habit" could never be satisfied, so I would steal from anyone, and I mean anyone! Finally, three years later, I was desperate. I believed I was on a count-down from ten to one and I was on number two: the end was upon me. It was only at this point that I knew I had to do something about my problem, so I 'phoned Clouds House (a treatment centre) and within three hours I was walking through the doors.

'I sat down, terrified, but felt that I was with people who understood all the dreadful things I had done, that I did not want to do, but simply could not stop myself doing. Since that day I have not looked back – except in astonishment. I chose to go 100% for recovery and am still in the process of doing just that.

'The twelve steps of the Alcoholics Anonymous programme are working for me and indeed work for others each and every day. Life has taken on a new meaning and whatever it is, I want it. I have never felt this good about myself in my whole life and I will let nothing take this feeling away.

'I am looking forward to being a responsible member of society and with the help of Alcoholics Anonymous and Narcotics Anonymous I will achieve this one day at a time.'

The scale of heroin use has been somewhat exaggerated, but more people are becoming users. The heroin trade is well organised and makes a great deal of money for those involved in supply. This commercial fact, coupled with the demand from users, means that it will be around for years to come.

Barbiturates and tranquillisers

Barbiturates have been used medically to calm people down and help them sleep. Most of them are produced as powders and are commonly sold made up into coloured capsules. They are taken by mouth, occasionally with alcohol, and it is possible to inject them. They are legally available only on a doctor's prescription. They depress the central nervous system in the same way as alcohol and produce similar effects. Large doses can produce unconsciousness and eventually death. Fatal overdose is an ever present danger as the required amount is very near the normal dose – just ten barbiturate pills can be enough. These effects and hazards will be magnified if alcohol has also been consumed.

Like barbiturates, tranquillisers are used to control anxiety and tension, to sedate and to help induce sleep. Benzodiazepines are the most commonly prescribed type and include Valium, Librium and Ativan. Because they are much safer, the benzodiazepines have replaced barbiturates for most medical purposes and are taken orally. They do not appear to be injected by drug abusers to any great extent. Like barbiturates, tranquillisers are available by prescription only.

Tranquillisers depress mental activity and attention but, in general, do not cause people to either feel lethargic or behave awkwardly, as do barbiturates. Nevertheless, skills such as driving are impaired and, as with alcohol, aggression is released as inhibitions are lowered. Far more tranquillisers than barbiturates need to be taken for a fatal overdose to result. Tranquillisers alone rarely produce the euphoria usually associated with either barbiturates, or alcohol. Indeed, this could account for their lack of popularity as 'recreational drugs' compared to barbiturates!

Tolerance to tranquillisers does develop as a result of long-term use and research has shown that withdrawal effects may result even with medically prescribed dosages. These, though not as serious as for barbiturates, can be unpleasant and protracted. They include insomnia, anxiety and nausea and, after unusually high doses, convulsions and mental confusion. Because the withdrawal syndrome can resemble the original complaint, both patient and doctor may continue the treatment. Physical dependence may then develop.

Psychological dependence can also develop with tranquillisers and people may feel confused, irritable or anxious and unable to carry on with their normal routine unless they continue taking the drug.

Amphetamines

Amphetamines are synthetic powders formed into a variety of tablets, capsules, etc, for medical use, sometimes in combination with other drugs. They are now recommended only for the treatment of pathological sleepiness and, paradoxically, hyperactivity in children. In the past they were widely prescribed for depression and appetite suppression.

Amphetamines are available by prescription only. Amphetamine sulphate powder is relatively easy to produce and large quantities are available illegally. Although amphetamines may be taken by mouth, dissolved in water, injected or even smoked, the powders are usually sniffed.

Amphetamines act in a similar way to the body's natural adrenalin. Breathing and heart rate speed up, the pupils widen and appetite lessens. Psychological dependence is a risk because they produce feelings of confidence and cheerfulness. As energy is burnt up the predominant feeling will become anxiety tinged with irritability and restlessness. High doses, especially when frequently repeated over several days, can produce delirium, panic, hallucinations or feelings of persecution. To maintain the desired effect a user has to take increasing doses.

Heavy use will merely postpone fatigue and hunger and not satisfy the need for rest and nourishment. It also risks damaging blood vessels and causing heart failure, especially amongst people who already have a high blood pressure or heart rate and also those who take strenuous exercise whilst using the drug.

Caffeine

Although caffeine is found in coffee, tea and soft drinks as well as chocolate, it is worth remembering that it is a stimulant which is an ingredient in a number of proprietary pain killers. It is possible to become dependent on caffeine and 'withdrawal' will bring headaches, drowsiness and irritability. Excessive use can cause anxiety and insomnia but there is no reliable evidence of lasting health damage from long-term use.

Caffeine can become a red herring in discussions about drugs (because of the novelty involved in even considering it) and can divert attention from the major problem areas.

Cocaine

Cocaine is a powerful stimulant derived from the coca plant which is grown mainly in South America. In its pure form it is highly poisonous. It can produce both physical and psychological dependence through regular use.

Usually coke is sniffed through a tube and if used regularly can severely damage the nasal passages. It can also be smoked in the form of crack. Either form is highly addictive. Crack is a major problem in many American cities and there are signs of its growing use in Britain. Produced from cocaine by a simple process, the name derives from the 'crackling' sound made when smoked. Crack became the media's favourite drug in the late 1980s although, like heroin and solvent abuse before, its use was exaggerated and sensationalised.

Sometimes coke is combined with heroin (a depressant drug) to prolong the 'high'. Alcohol may also be drunk at the same time to try and enhance the effects. But mixing drink with other drugs is dangerous because of the unpredictable results.

Once used as a painkiller and local anaesthetic for nose and throat operations, cocaine is being replaced in medical usage because of its addictive properties. The faster a drug is absorbed into the bloodstream the shorter the experience it produces. Cocaine has a brief but intense effect whilst the effect of a single dose of amphetamine may last for up to four hours. In order to stay high on cocaine, users may have to repeat their fix once or twice every hour.

Hallucinogenic drugs

LSD (lysergic acid diethylamide) is a synthetic white powder. Although it is well known, possibly because of its association with 'Flower Power' and hippies in the 1960s, its use has been limited since then. Its effects depend very much on the user's mood and often include intensified colours and other sight or sound distortions combined with the feeling of raised self-awareness. A feeling of being outside one's body is commonly reported. Unpleasant reactions may include depression, dizziness and sometimes panic. Deaths due to hallucinations, though much publicised in its heyday, are rare.

LSD and other chemical hallucinogens became fashionable in the late 1980s. The reappearance of LSD was linked with a new drug called 'Ecstasy' or MDMA. In 1988, *The Observer* newspaper described a new music fashion called 'acid house' which was linked with what it called a 'new psychedelia'. In fact, 'Ecstasy' was synthesised as long ago as 1914 but only became a street drug in the United States in the early 1980s. The drug has been shown to damage nerve paths in the brains of monkeys, but its use by humans is too recent to show up conclusive proof of brain damage.

'Magic mushrooms' is a general label for several species of mushrooms which can have hallucinogenic effects when eaten. About a dozen types grow wild in Britain and distinguishing them from poisonous varieties requires considerable knowledge. None of the mushrooms are subject to legal restrictions in themselves, although boiling or crushing them is illegal. Their effects are similar to a mild LSD experience but also include euphoria and hilarity. Unpleasant experiences can result but by far the biggest risk is the possibility of picking a poisonous species by mistake. Some of these can cause death even in small amounts.

Other drugs

It is impossible to cover every drug in one book. Fashions change, and experimentation produces new 'designer' drugs which may or may not become widely used. The market is driven partly by demand from the users and partly by the suppliers' search for greater profits. In many ways new 'products' may undermine established 'sales' and be an opportunity for increased income. For up-to-date information on the developing drug scene contact one of the organisations listed in Appendix 2.

Having looked briefly at the drugs which affect our society, we need to look at the other half of the 'drug problem' – the people who are at risk.

3

People at risk

Drug abuse is only one of a series of problems in human society. People take drugs in situations which are part of complex patterns of human behaviour. Sorting out the origin of a drug problem in the midst of other problems can be like asking whether the chicken or the egg came first. However, it will help us if we have an awareness of the 'risk factors'. We may then be able to prevent problems in the first place or, at least, help understand them better when trying to solve them.

Young people

Most young people start their drug usage with tobacco or alcohol and their introduction is often being offered a smoke or a drink by a friend, parent or someone else they know well. I can remember vividly my first – and last! – liqueur chocolate. I was offered it during a family Christmas when I was seven or eight years old. I bit it in half and it dripped onto my hitherto spotless white shirt! Family reaction ensured the memory! Similarly, I was in family surroundings when I was first offered home-made wine.

The family setting in which children first find out about and experience drugs (medicinal and others) will form opinions and habits. But for teenagers as parental control wanes, peer pressure takes over. Acting big in front of friends and impressing the opposite sex becomes important. Holding a cigarette feels good and the drug effect of nicotine soothes away any nervousness.

Advertising, too, has a powerful effect. Positive images like strength, good looks and virility are common themes which run through the promotion of tobacco and alcohol products. The British drinks industry spends over £200 million on advertising each year. The 'trade' argues that advertising persuades people to buy particular brands and does not influence overall consumption. Common sense, however, suggests that the persuasive power of advertising increases consumption. Even if we accept that advertising has no impact on overall consumption for existing consumers, we still have to ask what effect it has on young people.

A survey of alcohol promotion on television reported in the *British Medical Journal* concluded that 'the extent and influence of the promotion of alcohol were great and that such advertising is seen by many children and adolescents.' The survey found that over 12% of television advertising (in the winter of 1986/7) concerned alcoholic drinks. More worrying was the distribution of the advertising, with it being evenly balanced before and after 9 pm. Remember that many drinkers will be in their 'locals' for much of this time and so it is people who do not drink regularly (in pubs) who are the target audience. Advertisements for alcohol are highly professional, persuasive, glamorous and are often very funny or carry sexual or sporting overtones.

Tobacco advertising has been severely curtailed and there is a lobby which regards alcohol advertising as being too persuasive, especially for the young, and therefore requiring similar treatment. Public concern led the Government to rule, in the late 1980s, that nobody aged under twenty-five should appear in alcohol advertisements.

Advertising on television is only one factor in considering the media 'assault' on young people – or anybody else, for that matter. Drink and tobacco advertising appears in the cinema, magazines and newspapers as well as on posters. Sponsorship of sporting events offer tobacco companies massive exposure despite the television ban on advertising their products. Snooker, cricket and motor racing have been among those televised sports whose links with tobacco sponsorship have generated household names of tobacco brands. The drink trade also sponsors events. No wonder the European Commission proposed, in 1991, the introduction of new rules to control such sponsorship.

Concern about the influence of television on drinking habits – and young people's habits in particular – has traditionally focused on advertising. However, a look at TV drama and other entertainment has shown that scenes showing characters drinking alcohol take up twenty-five times as much air time as advertisements. This analysis appeared in *Brewing Review* in 1988 and made the point that this larger message content needs to be considered as well as the non-television factors such as peer pressure, parental attitudes and formal education. Soap operas are a major part of British television and this analysis showed that 'drinking scenes' constituted 14% of British productions, and only 10% and 6%, respectively, of American and Australian soaps. Do we all really spend as much time in pubs as the regulars at 'The Rovers Return', 'The Woolpack' or 'The Queen Vic'? Assessing the influence of television on drinking habits is not a clear cut issue and it is difficult to measure the effect which programmes have, especially as they are part of the wider set of influences already mentioned. Research in the United States has led to a suggestion that while television may not directly cause people to drink, it may cultivate ignorance about the potentially harmful effects – because it concentrates on drinking as a pleasant sociable activity.

Although no objective conclusion can yet be drawn about the effects of the mass media on young people's drinking habits, the evidence suggests that it must play a part in forming attitudes and the mainly one-sided approach to alcohol must have some influence. The observations of many parents would tend to support this.

Society does, of course, make some attempts to limit the use of alcohol and tobacco by the young. It is illegal to sell tobacco to anyone under sixteen and alcohol sales are forbidden to those under eighteen – or under sixteen if they are ordering a drink with a meal.

Alcohol problems among young people are not new. The Home Office's standing conference on crime prevention set up a working group which issued a report in November 1987 entitled *Young people and alcohol*. In it they noted that 350 children aged twelve and under were found drunk and incapable on the streets of Liverpool in 1877.

This report highlights a survey of alcohol consumption by young people carried out by the Office of Population Census and Surveys (OPCS). It shows the link between young people drinking alcohol from an early age with the availability of drink at home, although it does not indicate the degree to which the young people's drinking is under parental control. 82% of thirteen-year-old boys and 76% of thirteen-year-old girls (in England and Wales) were reported to have had a 'proper drink'. Three-quarters of all thirteen year olds said they usually drank at home compared to just under 30% who said they drank at parties. Obviously some of them drink in several places.

A second feature of the survey was that licensed premises were shown to be an important source of alcohol for young people under the age of eighteen. Even allowing for some exaggeration by the young people questioned it showed there was a lot of under-age drinking. 19% of thirteen-year-old boys said that they usually drank alcohol in a pub or a bar. This compared with 71% of the same group who said they usually drank alcohol at home. For boys aged seventeen the figures are 68% usually drinking in a pub or a bar and 25% at home. In reality, it is difficult to enforce the law on under-age drinking. Many discos have bars and 'under-age' young people patronise them. Even if they appear too young to buy for themselves, many will be able to persuade someone older to help them.

There are also legal provisions controlling the sale of tobacco. Those under sixteen years should not be sold any tobacco product. In practice, this law is as easily broken as are the alcohol restrictions. Shopkeepers do not always ask questions, and when they do, children may say that the cigarettes are for an adult – an excuse which does not make the sale legal.

As young people push against social barriers and explore the world and their own identity, they can develop a rebellious approach. This means that law-breaking has its own thrills, making drugs even more attractive. Illegal drugs may not be as widely available as alcohol and tobacco but law enforcement has not stopped their use.

Employment

Some jobs carry higher risks (statistically) than others that employees will become drug dependent, because of the nature of the work or the social traditions surrounding them. This is particularly true where alcohol abuse is concerned. No one should be surprised to see publicans at the top of a list of high-risk professions.

The top twenty occupations with the highest rate of death from cirrhosis of the liver – a disease caused by alcohol consumption in four out of five cases – are (starting with the worst): publicans; deck officers, engineering officers and ship's pilots; barstaff; barge and boatmen; fishermen; hotel managers; insurance brokers and financial agents; restaurateurs; drivers; cooks; shunters and pointsmen; mine workers; electrical engineers; journalists and authors; medical practitioners; garage proprietors; railway workers; maids, valets and related service workers; tobacco workers; metallurgists.

Some of the common work-associated causes of alcohol related problems are:

- strain and stress from hazards, work loads, responsibility or sexual harassment.
- availability of alcohol – for example, distillery workers, bar staff, sales staff and catering workers may find it easier to drink at work. Breweries have made bonus payments in the form of tokens to be exchanged for drink. Jobs involving entertaining clients will encourage drinking.
- isolation or separation – this can be a problem for shift workers, travelling workers, offshore workers and seafarers.
- facilities at work – more people will drink at meal breaks if canteen facilities are poor and if alcohol is on sale at the workplace or nearby.
- a tradition of 'after work' or lunchtime trips to a pub.

Some areas and jobs have reputations for hard drinking and a mixture of local and work cultures can combine to give an increased incidence of alcohol related problems.

Stress

Stress is a well-publicised fact of modern life and all of us suffer from it to some degree. Bereavement, divorce, marital problems and redundancy all cause severe stress. Caring for young children or older relatives often makes such demands on the carers – usually women – that they neglect their own physical, emotional and creative needs and raise their stress levels.

Family doctors are often the first line of defence against stress related problems. Tranquillisers can reduce crippling anxiety or help a person sleep in a time of crisis, but, as we have seen, there are dangers of dependency.

The American Food and Drug Administration ruled in 1980 that all prescriptions for drugs like Valium should be accompanied by a leaflet pointing out the dangers. One such leaflet reads:

> You can become dependent on Valium. Dependence is a craving for the drug or the inability to function normally without it. An overdose of Valium alone or with other drugs can be fatal. You should avoid drinking alcohol while taking Valium.
>
> A combination of alcohol and tranquillisers dangerously increases the effects of both. Studies suggest an increased rate of birth defects in children whose mothers took Valium during the first three months of pregnancy. If you have been taking Valium for a month or more your doctor should reassess your condition and your continued use of the drug. The effect of these drugs for the relief of anxiety for periods longer than four months has not been studied.

Doctors are aware of the potential dangers, but the pressures on them, and the expectations of their patients, can often mean that a drug route to a 'solution' of the problem is the most acceptable.

People do not always turn to doctors for help with stress and will use social drugs to alleviate a situation. Benzodiazepines have to be supplied on prescription, but cigarettes and alcoholic drinks can be bought on demand. Taking a drink to calm the nerves or puffing at a cigarette is the only way many people can cope with life. Think about the response of the people you know – how do they cope in moments of stress? Some of us eat, rather than drinking or smoking. But shouldn't Christians be reaching out for God's peace, and encouraging others to do the same? Regrettably, this is sometimes easier said than done.

Older people

Older people are also an 'at risk' group. In this case the danger may arise from the medical use of drugs. Older people will often require different types of medication and may get confused about which pills and potions have to be taken on what days and at what time intervals. Little boxes can be used to sort out the pills into different days, but anyone who has tried to steer an elderly relative through a drug regime will know how complicated it gets.

Older people are more vulnerable to the effects of alcohol on their prescribed medications. Those most likely to cause difficulties include painkillers; antihistamines (often found in cough mixtures); antibiotics; and prescriptions for rheumatism, depression, arthritis, sleeplessness, diabetes, anxiety, high blood pressure, epilepsy, blood-clots and thrombosis (anti-coagulants). Although this may seem a long list, it does not cover all conditions and anyone taking medicines should check with their doctor to see if alcohol will have any effect. Some medicines that are readily available over the counter of a chemist's shop should *not* be mixed with alcohol. These include some of the medicines for headaches, cough mixtures, travel sickness pills, etc.

Alcohol agencies consider that we do not fully appreciate the extent of the risk for older people. They are under-represented on the agencies' case loads and there are a number of reasons which may account for this. For example, older people may find it difficult to travel to offices, climb stairs or use the telephone. Older people may feel more embarrassed at discussing their problems with younger people and will feel that alcohol problems carry a heavy stigma.

Tolerance to alcohol decreases with age, partly because the liver and kidneys become less efficient and so may be slower to remove alcohol from the body. Shakiness, trembling, confusion, loss of memory and incontinence are associated with old age and regarded as 'incurable'. Alcohol can, however, produce these symptoms – and its removal can alleviate them. Those working with older people should be aware that 'old age' is not necessarily the cause of every health problem.

If Christians want to help people then it is helpful to identify factors which make an individual at risk. Prevention is better than cure, and the realisation that changed circumstances can lead to changed habits may just make that difference necessary to see someone through a crisis. Membership of an 'at risk' group does not automatically indicate a problem, but it will make one more likely – statistically. In the last analysis, we are all at some risk.

4

A Christian response?

The only drug mentioned in the Bible is alcohol, and different interpretations of the texts have led to considerable argument and division in the past. Discussions about whether or not to drink have obscured a need for all Christian people to work together to help those suffering.

There is very little information about how, and to what extent, Christians use alcohol. A Methodist Division of Social Responsibility survey into attitudes and usage among lay people, conducted in 1982, indicated that a substantial majority of Methodists occasionally drank. The frequency of alcohol use was somewhat below the national average and there was a significant minority who were teetotal. Those who responded to the survey claimed that their attitudes to and use of alcohol had not changed significantly over time. There was some indication from the survey that attitudes to alcohol vary according to age: those in the older age groups were more likely to be opposed to alcohol use and to be abstainers.

The question of 'drinking' arouses strong – and contrary – feelings for Christians. Alcohol is a depressant drug and yet wine receives commendation in the Bible! Wine has been used throughout the history of the Christian church and of Judaism. For example, Exodus 29: 40 records that the 'fourth part of a hin of wine' (probably about 1½ pints) formed a drink offering. Genesis 9: 20 refers to Noah becoming a farmer and planting the first recorded vineyard. (Later he became drunk, which in turn led to serious family problems.) Jesus' first miracle was to turn water into wine at the wedding feast in Cana (John 2) and Timothy was advised by Paul to take some wine for his stomach's sake, presumably for medicinal purposes (1 Timothy 5: 23).

Christianity is not alone in its acceptance of alcoholic drinks. Wine and beer have been used as offerings to deities of many kinds, and sometimes as a means of enabling priests to reach a state of ecstasy or frenzy.

Although there are over 600 references to drink and drinking in the Bible, Christians have been unable to interpret them with one mind.

The majority of biblical references can be found in the Old Testament. Isaiah complained: 'Priests and prophet stagger from beer and are befuddled with wine; they reel from beer, they stagger when seeing visions, they stumble when rendering decisions. All the tables are covered with vomit and there is not a spot without filth' (Isaiah 28: 7,8).

Proverbs contains a lot of advice and comment about drink. Chapter 20 starts with the statement: 'Wine is a mocker and beer a brawler; whoever is led astray by them is not wise.' Proverbs 23: 29–35 vividly describes drunkenness, and chapter 31: 4–7 seems to suggest that leaders should be teetotal whilst the poor may be allowed to drink to forget their poverty! (The writer is probably using irony to highlight the needs of the poor.)

Daniel abstained from the king's wine and emerged as someone fit to hold high office. Hosea writes about 'old wine and new, which take away the understanding of my people' (4: 11). Besides Noah, specific examples of alcohol misuse can be found in 2 Samuel 11 (David and Uriah), 2 Samuel 13 (Absalom and Amnon) and 1 Kings 16 (Zimri and Elah).

Yet alongside much that is negative, the Bible has positive words about 'wine that gladdens the heart of man' (Psalm 104: 15). And some commendation may be implied in the use of wine as a drink offering – since surely God would command only acceptable sacrifices.

The late nineteenth and early twentieth centuries were times when scholars produced all sorts of tracts and booklets promoting their point of view. The temperance movement leant heavily on 'proof-texts' from the Old Testament. At times they could be criticised for ignoring the context as they sought to persuade Christians to become total abstainers. Apart from the danger of taking verses out of context (see the Proverbs 31: 4–7 passage referred to earlier) the whole approach became like a contest where texts were thrown at each other by drinking and non-drinking Christians. This was an era when barriers between Christians were built and which gave the temperance movement an image which lingers among many Christians today. Those who used alcohol in moderation were able to take the 'moral high ground' of the New Testament for some of their best quotes, like the wedding at Cana. Paul did not appear to condemn drink, and in Timothy's case positively recommended it!

The temperance lobby countered with the view that there was confusion caused by the translation of Hebrew and Greek words as 'wine'. Apparently Hebrew distinguishes between fermented and alcohol-free drinks and Greek doesn't. Although this might make individual texts clearer it does not alter the fact that many Jews and early Christians in Bible times drank wine. With care, texts may be used in isolation, but as far as drink is concerned there is a lot more to consider before reaching a conclusion. The situation is further complicated when we consider drugs other than alcohol, since we have to decide if the references to drink apply to other drugs. If the moderate use of alcohol is biblically sanctioned, then would this apply to substances which, it is arguable, are less risky than alcohol – like some solvents and cannabis? To answer this question, four factors have to be considered:

1 what the Bible teaches about Christian living;
2 possible differences between the modern world and biblical times;
3 our historical legacy;
4 our view of what Jesus would do in our situation.

Christian lifestyle

Jesus told the story of the Good Samaritan to help his listeners understand the meaning of the command to 'love your neighbour as yourself'. Our response to God's unconditional love should be an openness to others. There are no limits on those for whom we should show love and concern – we should be prepared to help others no matter who they are or what their situation. This parable shows care in action as the Samaritan tends the victim. But, of course, care can also operate to prevent the problem arising in the first place!

Paul writes about positive examples when he states that people should not do anything that might encourage other people to do wrong. 'Be careful, however, that the exercise of your freedom does not become a stumbling-block to the weak' (1 Corinthians 8: 9). 'Therefore, if what I eat causes my brother to fall into sin, I will never eat meat again, so that I will not cause him to fall' (1 Corinthians 8: 13). *We* may be safe, but is our example harmful to others? For instance, what about a minister seen drinking at a wedding? If he drives home, what message is he giving out? Even if he does not drive, will his example encourage others to drink and drive? These represent important questions, not simply for ministers but for all of us.

Times of celebration are occasions when we all have an opportunity to make a statement about alcohol abuse, at little personal cost. A decision to 'stay dry' might encourage others to follow suit and reduce the risk of alcohol related incidents that, sadly, can mar celebrations.

And what sort of example do we give young people, our colleagues and family? Many Christians are only very moderate drinkers, but we have to ask whether that goes far enough in a world where alcohol is linked to so much misery. The Christian is expected to have a lifestyle which will glorify God.

God, our creator, designed the human body, and it is therefore important that our bodies should be kept fit and healthy. Abuse of our bodies undermines any attempt to live as Christ would want. Such abuse is tantamount to insulting God because it damages his creation. And because our bodies are the temple of the Spirit (1 Corinthians 3: 16) and we are to be filled with the Spirit (Ephesians 5: 18) it follows that any use of drugs which adversely affects the body must weaken our relationship with Christ.

We are part of our society and are caught up in all its social problems – of which the drugs issue is only one. We need to see it in this wider context and apply biblical principles to our daily living in order to develop a lifestyle which is authentically Christian.

Bible times

The strongest source of instruction about Christian lifestyle is Jesus himself. If the Bible recorded categorically that Jesus unequivocably condemned drink then we would be in a very clear position with regard to total abstinence. However, there is no such record and Jesus' first miracle can be taken to suggest that wine is God-given and should be enjoyed as such.

There has been much speculation about the sort of wine Jesus produced at the wedding in Cana. Some have suggested that it was non-alcoholic. There is certainly logic in the suggestion that Jesus would not have wanted to make the guests more merry and, therefore, more likely to do silly things – especially as the Old Testament warns against drunkenness! But there is no indication in the text that this was or was not the case.

There are no grounds to conclude that Jesus was a total abstainer and, given the social situation, it is probable that he would have drunk the mildly alcoholic wine of his time. This is reinforced by Jesus' comments in Luke 7: 33, 34 where he compares John the Baptist's abstinence with his own 'eating and drinking'. Another factor to consider is that sanitation was poor and a low alcohol content wine would be a safer drink than some of the water. This may have been the reason for Paul's advice to Timothy to take some wine for his stomach's sake (1 Timothy 5: 23).

The nature of life in Bible times reduced the risks associated with alcohol consumption. In a world without cars, drinking was potentially less dangerous, and the nature of community life meant that few people were in a position to become secret drinkers. 'Communications' were not as well developed as they are today and there was no advertising to influence behaviour. Today, a multi-million pound industry invests a great deal to persuade people to drink and smoke. And television soaps and serials constantly portray drinking as something everyone does.

Jesus dealt with matters that were directly relevant to his time. Many of the drug problems we face were unknown in his day. The Bible makes no comment about drugs, and no clear instructions are given because it simply was not an issue. The fact that the Bible cannot be used as a simple rule book makes it all the more important, as we have already seen, that we strive to apply biblical principles and develop a Christian lifestyle.

Our historical legacy

The 'lifestyle' principles are helpful, but Christians have still not avoided controversy about drink and its place within the church. The past is often the key to the present and another brief look at the temperance movement will help explain some of the reasons for a lack of late twentieth-century Christian action on alcohol abuse.

Many people, some Christian and some not, became very concerned with early nineteenth-century alcohol abuse and formed what became known as 'Temperance Societies'. For the first part of the nineteenth century they aimed to encourage a reduction in alcohol problems by agreeing to drink moderately, a policy similar to that adopted by most health agencies today.

By the 1830s this approach was not bringing success, and breakaway 'Total Abstinence Societies' were formed. Many people had decided to avoid alcohol completely because they felt a personal stand was necessary as an example for others. Soon the old temperance (moderation) societies dwindled and the total abstinence movement became known as the temperance movement. Much of this was Christian based and went ahead with considerable enthusiasm, seeing an enormous growth in membership during the rest of the century. The Band of Hope started with one children's group in Leeds in 1847 and had three and a half million children and adults as members by 1900. Thomas Cook started his travel firm to show that 'dry' day trips were enjoyable and that drink was not essential to having a good time.

There were other social issues in nineteenth century Britain, and many great Christian reformers were at work in education, health or other forms of social welfare. The temperance movement was an important part of this Victorian social reform. Despite 'converting' many people to their cause, the movement also gave rise to division between Christians, as some continued to drink moderately.

The temperance organisations were very committed to win children and young people for Christ and did not see their role as merely being 'anti-booze' agencies. A typical motto from Kingswood, near Bristol, was 'To win the young for Christ and total abstinence'. Evangelism and social action went hand in hand. Thousands became Christians because of the movement.

Its demise did not occur until the twentieth century when Britain had become a more sober place and there was less obvious evidence of drink-related problems. Fashion, a change in emphasis by the brewers' advertising (they began directing it at young people in the 1930s), a lack of awareness of alcohol problems and the intransigence of many of the temperance societies combined to lead to changes in society.

The pendulum started to swing back towards 'social drinking' and more Christians felt that there was nothing wrong with the occasional glass. After all, the Anglican and Catholic churches had not really embraced the temperance movement and throughout this period wine had continued to be used in communion services and celebrations.

What would Jesus do?

Most Christians would state categorically that Jesus would not take illegal drugs or sniff solvents. Many Christians, particularly in recent years, would be surprised to see a twentieth-century Jesus smoking tobacco. The question then becomes very specific and drink-related. Given the evidence of social harm, the biblical emphasis on personal fitness and public example, what do you think Jesus would do today?

Much of the emphasis of Jesus' teaching and parables is focused upon a correct attitude towards God, other people and things or possessions. Read, for example, the story of the faithful servant (Matthew 24); the 'salt and light' teaching (Matthew 5); the story of the rich fool (Luke 12) and the story of the two housebuilders (Matthew 7). Try to think about the implications for alcohol and other drug use in all these stories. Then consider many of Jesus' miracles. He is concerned with wholeness and harmony, both in individual lives and in social relationships. Consider the effects of alcohol and other drugs upon the mind and body and examine whether the use of depressants or stimulants does or does not encourage life in all its fullness. Finally, remember that Jesus instructed us to love others – in practical ways – and warned us about the dangers of putting obstacles in the way of their spiritual development.

An alcohol-free lifestyle should not be seen as an overreaction. The Bible is quite clear that this was an acceptable practice for some. And sometimes a clear-cut example is needed if concern is to be demonstrated.

A Christian response?

Our response must have personal and public dimensions. Publicly we can get involved in helping others – by prevention and cure – but to do this effectively each of us needs to understand our own drug use and be able to reason out whether we should change our habits. We can very easily send out confusing signals and anyone seeking to help a substance abuser needs a reply to the response, 'Well, you drink, don't you?!'

Similarly, anyone who chooses not to drink needs to be sufficiently open-minded to understand that people make their own choices. Total abstinence may not be the only authentically Christian response.

A prayerful and open mind will set each of us on the road to God's answer. This chapter gives no clear, simple answer – deliberately – and leaves it up to each one of us to decide what he or she should do.

5

. . . *In the home*

Immediately the idea of actually responding to drug problems is raised, many of us will shy away because we have no first-hand experience. Perhaps we may think about 'rescuing the perishing' or just not know how to start – even if we wanted to begin. As Christians we live in different environments. We will look at ways of responding in each one. Our home life is the place to start.

Influence on children

Home life is the primary influence on children as they grow up. Christians place a high value on a strong and loving family life and want to see children accept Jesus for themselves. Parental example may well be a major factor in this.

The OPCS survey referred to earlier showed it was the availability of alcohol in the home that was a major influence in shaping a young person's drinking habits. The same is true for smoking. Adult life reflects the attitudes formed and lessons learnt in childhood. Habits picked up from parents will almost unconsciously be used when dealing with one's own children. To change them for the better requires a lot of will power and determination, although to change them for the worse does not!

One of the common questions asked by parents is,

'What should I do if my son/daughter sniffs glue or smokes or is found drunk?' But, as in so many areas of life, prevention is better than cure. We should think about what can be done to reduce the opportunity for the problem to arise in the first place.

Equipping children to choose

It is important to help children develop the skills for making right choices. In their early years children have choices made for them. Teachers and parents choose what they may do and then tell them to get on with it. This has to happen or anarchy would reign at home and in school, but it is a situation which does not give much scope to practise choice.

As they grow, children face a wider variety of choices. They should be encouraged to judge for themselves. The use of controlled choice as a means of helping children to practise judgment will vary according to age and subject, but here are some situations which illustrate the point. (You ought to be able to think of plenty more.)

1 Your eight-year-old son has been given some money. You would like him to spend it on Lego Technic but he would like a Teenage Mutant Hero Turtle. What do you say to him?
2 Breakfast time. Do you offer your three year old a choice of cereals? Always? Sometimes? Never!
3 Buying clothes. How much choice do you permit? At what age!?
4 What choice of drinks do you allow at Christmas and other celebrations?
5 Do you vet children's choices of who to invite to a birthday party?
6 Who chooses what to do on holiday?
7 Church attendance. At what age is there any choice?
8 Do you persist in serving children 'good' food in the hope they will eventually choose to eat it?

There is often no single 'right answer' to how much choice can be offered to a child, but if none is ever available then he or she will be less able to face the world. It is important, whatever happens, to keep open the lines of communication. Children may not always do what we would like, but as long as we listen and try to understand them there will be opportunities to help and support them.

Moving specifically to our theme, alcohol is the drug most likely to be found at home. The opportunity to choose what to drink is worth thinking through. For example, Christmas is a time when families get together and enjoy themselves. Many will have wine on their table and have to decide whether and at what age children should be allowed to drink. Let us assume that there is some concern about giving them alcohol to drink, and that something non-alcoholic is provided – like orange squash. The children see their parents and relatives drinking wine from attractive stem glasses while they are drinking orange squash from glass or plastic tumblers. What sort of image are they receiving? Inevitably they will ask for wine because they want to imitate their parents. The same applies to beers and spirits.

There will be a range of parental responses which start with,'You are not old enough', go on to a detailed attempt to explain why they should not be drinking alcohol, and conclude with, 'Yes, just a little one.'

However, more positive steps could be taken. Children could be given the same glasses and they could have some more attractive alcohol-free drinks – there are plenty of grape and other juices available these days. (Children usually prefer fruit juices because they're sweeter.) So far, so good. The adults have provided attractive drinks for their children. However, at the moment there is little choice being demonstrated until some of the adults show that the children's drinks are also worthwhile – by having some for themselves. Certainly parents should think very carefully before providing alcoholic drinks for children, and not do so at all until children are able to make responsible choices *and* cope with the consequences.

What should adults who are teetotallers do? Should they provide wine or other alcoholic drinks? Certainly they should think it through, but there are already plenty of images which come over *via* television, advertising and other means which show children an attractive side to drink. Parents do not need to feel that the only way of providing their children with genuine choice is to provide alcohol.

Those who do provide alcoholic drinks should remember that the effect of alcohol on a child is much greater than for an adult. The drug effect of alcohol also encourages further consumption – perhaps to the extent of raiding opened bottles of wine! Parents need to be careful about where they keep their drinks and cigarettes. If they are accessible to children then there will always be a risk that the 'invitation' will be taken up.

Hidden influences

The media exert a powerful influence on the image of drinking and smoking. Newspapers and magazines are full of advertisements. Television does have additional controls, like the ban on cigarette advertising and a code of practice for drinks promotions. However, drinks advertising is 'small beer' when compared to the amount of time given over to sponsored sport or drinking scenes in programmes like 'Eastenders'.

'Grange Hill' may have its critics, but it has tried to deal with heroin quite positively. Apart from the story line, the cast were involved in a 'Say No' video which was given a lot of air time. Saying No was criticised as being a 'negative encouragement' to try drugs, but it was a lively, positive performance that could be extended to apply to other drugs besides heroin. Another of the

'Grange Hill' story lines showed the school bully in trouble because of his drinking.

Whatever we do – being selective in our viewing or choosing not to have a television – we cannot remove the influence of the media. Friends will still have their televisions and advertising is everywhere. Countering it is a long-term process and must be part of the general home atmosphere. There will be times when it is right to talk about drugs specifically, but it is what underlies the functioning of a home that counts. Christian parenthood should involve encouraging a healthy lifestyle and parental attitudes will be part of this general approach.

If parents are less than consistent in some areas then mixed messages will spill over into others. For example, do we take risks with ourselves and our families by driving too fast? Do we eat too much and miss out on 'healthy' foods? Do we take any exercise? What sort of 'silent example' do we put on show by our behaviour? Parenthood can seem like a burden as well as a minefield and the last thing I want to do is to introduce a checklist of 'good' parental behaviour. There are enough warts in my own behaviour to make me run a mile before offering myself as a model! However, I do know that dynamic, positive, Christian parenting offers the best chance to resolve issues before getting anywhere near a crisis. It also offers the best base from which to solve problems if and when they occur.

Home influences on drug use cannot be confined to straightforward copying, or even lifestyle generally. For example, home influences should enable children to learn to have confidence in themselves and their own abilities. A lack of self-esteem can have far-reaching consequences. I once met someone who felt insignificant when compared to an apparently more successful member of the family. Her answer was to use drink as a way of avoiding a confrontation with herself on this question of self-esteem. She came from a family which had connections with a church and which could be regarded as being 'ordinary', with no special needs. This kind of emotional deprivation is one example of a 'hidden influence' which can push people towards drug use – and abuse.

Parents may by now feel that I have concentrated too much on drink and not enough on the really dangerous drugs. I have done so because alcohol is the major drug in the home context.

Being positive

Having examined the provision of choice and the importance of other factors influencing children, like self-esteem, what else might parents do? Another step should be to understand their own position so that they can explain it in words that their children will understand. The scriptural principles of Christian living, which were discussed in Chapter 4, are essential here, but so is an understanding of the 'outside the home' environment. Basic information about drugs is also important. Although this book provides it, children and teenagers require a more visual presentation. A few leaflets kept at home would be an inexpensive and wise investment. They would also be helpful for discussing the subject with other parents.

We should avoid bcing ncgative. It is important to develop a positive Christian lifestyle. This includes looking at what the family eat and trying out 'healthy' food and drink. There is nothing wrong with enjoying what we eat and the cultivation of a good palate!

Dealing with problems

Despite the best home environment it is still impossible to guarantee that children will avoid drug-related problems. School and other activities will bring them into contact with substance abuse. So, what can a parent do when their child comes home drunk from a party, or is found sniffing glue?

It is important not to overreact. Any drug use has to be taken seriously, but the shouting and anger that can be caused by worry are not the best ways to find a solution. Tender, loving and persistent care is a foundation of good relationships and may have to be provided in great measure. Listening is an important skill, and picking up the upspoken messages as to 'why' is important. After all, drink and tobacco are used for reasons which may be as straightforward as enjoyment or more complicated if they relate to examination nerves or the loss of a boy or girl friend. Being 'chucked' is traumatic enough without a parent finding out that was why drink was an attractive refuge.

Children and teenagers will always experiment, and although any drug use involves risks it does not mean that there will be a long-term problem. If parents can learn something about the substances in common use then they will be in a position to discuss difficult problems (even if they do not come up for months or years) rather than leave them to the level of education available in the playground.

If problems do arise then the worst thing is for pride to prevent a search for help. Experimentation with any drug does not mean parental failure because children, like adults, are their own selves. It will not be necessary in every case to call out the counsellors and social workers, but there are organisations and individuals around who will give advice. Christian friends, if they know, can pray – but they have to be told first.

Suppose your teenage daughter comes home late from a party and has obviously been drinking. Remembering that this may be an isolated episode, how would you react? It *does* depend on the circumstances. Did you allow her to take a bottle and, if so, what did it contain? Was it a church 'do'? If it was at a friend's house, were there adults around to ensure all was well? Do you believe in providing transport home?

Remember, too, that it will be impossible to communicate effectively with someone who is 'under the influence' and worried about what you will do. It would be wrong to pay no attention to her state, but shouting will do no good. Would a cup of hot chocolate (ie doing something for her) break the ice and enable conversation? The following morning may be a better time to chat and find out if anything was wrong. After all, everyone else may have arrived home in that state and she would have been 'enjoying' herself like the others.

Even if your anxiety got the better of you and she went to bed with cross words being spoken, that is not the end of the world. Her lifetime will have been full of your 'bridge building' and it will be important to re-establish normal relationships as soon as possible. What you say depends on the ground work you have already done. Have you discussed alcohol and tobacco? What are your ground rules? Getting drunk is a regular pastime for some people, so that in one sense to be drunk is not unusual. There is no easy answer and the long-term solution rests in enabling children to be themselves and at the same time encouraging them to hold positive ideas about healthy Christian lifestyles.

The same principles apply to smoking, solvents or any other drug use. However a major hurdle will be to recognise substance abuse. Many parents take no action because they do not know their children are using a drug. Even when drug use is obvious, some parents may refuse to admit the symptoms and signs because *their* children would never do such a thing! But what are the signs?

Solvents may make a child listless and cause sores around the mouth and nose. If you found plastic bags or aerosol cans in their room or notice that some of your household products run out quickly, you will have cause to watch out. If money goes missing it may be being used on drink, cigarettes or solvents. Children may use their dinner money or walk home to save cash. Drink could disappear from your home stocks – the remainder might be diluted. Children also get access to these substances outside the home, but at least parents can observe on their own patch. Even so, it is impractical to lock up all potential substances, as one youth leader found when his young people took to sniffing the fumes of molten table tennis balls. Parents can talk to other parents too. Do not neglect opportunities to do this as mutual support can be very helpful.

Writing this chapter has made me acutely aware of my own failings as a father and reminded me that many homes do not have the type of relationship between parents and children which I have implied is desirable. This does not mean that nothing can be done, but highlights the fact that we all start from different positions. A child with no real parental support may more easily slip into drug use and take others along as well. However, children from Christian, secure families have opportunities to spread their security to others. Parents who have achieved a good family life need to be aware that it can be shared beyond their own children.

Although we have concentrated on home influences on children, adults will also be able to apply the principles to other relationships. For example, a choice of drinks would enable drivers to travel home safely. Christians have always used their homes for evangelism and fellowship and they give out powerful messages about lifestyle.

Each one of us makes our own decisions about what we do in our homes, and it is undeniable that we can use them in many ways for God's service. In doing so, we all have to account for the sort of 'open' or 'hidden' messages we give to others.

6

. . . At school or work

Everyone goes to school and then to youth training, work or college. Some may have spells when they are unemployed. These experiences are major influences in our lives and offer opportunities for Christian example and service.

We have already considered the statistical link between drink-related problems and some kinds of work, but school and college life also have associations with drug use. Smoking ('behind the bike sheds'), solvent abuse, and drinking (at lunch time) all figure as extra-curricular activities. Cannabis use is common in many areas, and dealers may mix it with heroin for smoking – so as to introduce a more expensive habit to school children. College life offers plenty of opportunity for drug use, particularly if a student has moved away from home.

Schools

Children are open to all sorts of pressures and influences about drugs even if they cannot legally purchase alcohol or tobacco for 'recreational' use. Sometimes these 'messages' get mixed up. Home, school, church and youth group may each tell different stories, none of which will be reflected in peer group experience.

Nearly everyone who starts using a drug does so because a friend introduced it to them. This is true for legally available and illegal drugs. And 'friend' can also mean a parent or someone else who is respected and admired. The picture of an evil pusher hiding behind a street corner waiting to pounce on an unsuspecting victim is largely untrue. Accuracy is important, particularly in drug education, which should neither minimise nor exaggerate the dangers of drug use. This has been recognised in many schools. Scare tactics may strengthen the conviction of those who are not going to take drugs anyway, but they will seem false when friends talk about their marvellous experiences and show no signs of being addicted or having physical ill-effects – perhaps because they have not taken that particular drug for long enough. The persuasive power of a friend's personal example will always be greater than information that appears exaggerated or untrue.

Alcohol and other drug education can turn up in different parts of the syllabus. Most secondary schools include it within their Personal, Social and Health Education (PSHE) programmes, and this has become a dynamic subject as teachers have worked to make it relevant to young people.

PSHE is a vital part of a school's programme and parents need to be aware of its existence and push to give it some priority. Although most teachers will do more than simply present the facts about drugs, there are different approaches and policy will vary from school to school. Most schools are aware of the need to make counselling time available to discuss problems and thereby provide a caring function as well as promote a healthy lifestyle.

In 1986 the Government made a special allocation of funds to enable education authorities to employ drug advisory teachers. Since then authorities have run courses to assist class teachers to carry out alcohol and drug education. Teachers first have to come to terms with their own attitudes and then inform, encourage and educate by challenging attitudes amongst young people and prompting them to work out their own solutions.

Teachers sometimes invite visiting speakers in, but the emphasis is on attempting to provide alcohol and drug education from within a school's own resources. Primary schools concentrate on the healthy living aspects of life; cleaning teeth, eating good food and so on because it is not appropriate to talk about specific drugs at early ages. This will be introduced as children get older – perhaps in the junior age group because there is a growing recognition that drug education has to be introduced before secondary school.

The direction taken in schools varies between the promotion of healthy living (which will emphasise the rights of individuals to choose whether or not to use a drug) and a policy based on 'harm reduction'. At its extreme, this latter style adopts the view that young people will inevitably experiment with drugs and therefore PSHE policy should be to equip them to do so as safely as possible. Harm reduction is a controversial approach, but it attempts to go beyond the unrealistic assumptions of a simple 'Say No' campaign. Some young people *will* use drugs whatever positive education has been undertaken. Telling them to stop immediately will be much less effective than encouraging them to use clean needles, drink in moderation and smoke low tar rather than high tar cigarettes. There is some logic behind the 'step at a time' approach which harm reduction can represent. Each of us has to make a judgment about its ethics, however, as opponents argue that it will encourage non-users to start using drugs because of the emphasis on 'safe use'. (Harm reduction is considered further in Appendix 7.)

Alcohol education has had its own version of 'harm reduction' in operation for some years. The concept of sensible drinking has been linked to the idea of safe limits – something that was touched upon in Chapter 2 when the strengths of alcoholic drinks were compared by using units of alcohol.

That's the Limit is a free leaflet that was produced by the Health Education Authority. Many copies were supplied to schools and used as a part of alcohol education. It contains valuable information, but its overwhelming emphasis is on encouraging people to drink sensibly. It sets its safe limits at 21 units per week for men and 14 units for women (ie the equivalent of 10.5 pints of average strength beer for men or 14 glasses of wine for women). These are primarily designed to encourage people to avoid long-term health problems and should not be applied to other related problems such as road accidents or crime. Small amounts of alcohol depress the brain sufficiently to increase the likelihood of these types of incidents.

The trouble with using this approach in schools is that the limits are designed for adults and were introduced as a means to encourage heavy drinkers to reduce their consumption. Teenagers may view them as permissible levels to which they can increase their drinking and, in addition, many of them will be under-age. Remember, too, that they will not yet be physically or emotionally fully mature. Safe limits started out as a 'harm reduction' technique but are now being applied as a general health education approach. Of course, many teachers will point out that the limits are designed for adults – but teenagers want full adulthood immediately. . . .

Harm reduction is not an easy issue to grapple with, because teenagers *do* use drugs of all sorts and for most heavy users abstinence is not a practical immediate answer. How should Christians react to harm reduction approaches – either as taught in school or applied outside? How can the moral dilemma of appearing to legitimise drug use be balanced against the practical desire to minimise harm?

Harm reduction is an approach which has implications for more than educational policy. One Christian magazine ran an article on drinking and said that the provision of taxis to take people home after parties was a good idea. This is an example of the harm reduction philosophy being recommended for use by Christians in the context of teenage parties.

The concept has a similar philosophical base to the Government's campaign for 'safe sex' to reduce the risk of HIV/AIDS. There has been controversy about the ethics of this. The policy is justified by its proposers who argue that it is unrealistic to encourage people to have one sexual partner. The objective is to make it safe to continue sleeping around. The possibility that people can be encouraged to limit their sexual activity to one partner is regarded as unrealistic as living an alcohol-free life. Yet millions of people have demonstrated that each of these positions are realistic.

Today, parents have increased rights to get involved in school life. The Government has provided for a degree of 'parent management' and it should be easier to make enquiries about a school's policy and the literature it uses. Does it only deal with personal health? Does it encourage people to avoid unsafe habits or does it offer ways of making them safer? Does it give emphasis to the effect that personal example has on other people?

Christian parents and governors could look for Christian-based material to recommend for use in schools. Recent experience has shown that schools are willing to buy large quantities of Band of Hope literature, for example, if they know of its existence. There is an openness today amongst teaching staff to consider resources on their merits – whatever the source. Health education literature must not be written as evangelistic material, but if it has been written from Christian principles then that is good.

Teachers also have an important place as role-models. What sort of example do they set on school trips? I can remember my two school rugby tours when staff allowed drinking and participated themselves. Today I have heard drinking teachers say that they no longer think that it is appropriate to allow this or to drink themselves – because of the power of their example. They were not Christians – just people who knew that what they did affected those for whom they were responsible.

What about Parent/Teacher Association raffles or functions? How many offer an alcoholic drink as a prize? Apart from being technically illegal (a licence is required to sell alcohol) what sort of message is given out to pupils sent home with raffle tickets to sell? There is plenty of television time which promotes alcoholic drinks as being the only choice without schools participating as well. PTA functions could be times when 'smoke-free' or 'dry' zones are invoked just to demonstrate that adults want to do something to show substance abuse is worth making a statement about. The principles considered by churches which have 'banned' alcohol from their premises apply here (see Chapter 9).

We have already looked at the influence of the home, and if school health education is to achieve anything then it has to take note of this. Mixed messages only cause confusion and schools should let parents know about their policies in this as well as other areas.

All health education policies should promote the idea of a 'healthy lifestyle' and this should mean ensuring that drug-free living is presented as fun. Schools could set up alcohol-free bars attached to their sports facilities. Giving teenagers practice in asking for non-alcoholic drinks will be important for their confidence if they are to do the same in a pub or family situation.

Higher education

Colleges and universities, unlike schools, are not places where alcohol and drug education can be timetabled in the curriculum. Different approaches are called for and churches which have students attending could encourage promoting a positive Christian lifestyle. Encouraging the adoption of Christian principles should not stop in Sunday school and the youth group. Something could be specially laid on for students.

Perhaps a church might consider what role it and its members could play at examination time when stresses rise and there are considerable temptations to relieve them by resorting to drink, cigarettes or other drugs. Members could provide opportunities for students to relax in their homes, giving support and encouragement. Such a policy can also help to deal with the loneliness often felt by some students which can lead to drinking or drug abuse.

Work

Young (and older) Christians at work will face pressures which they will not have experienced at home or school. Christmas parties are occasions when people get drunk – especially if the cost of the booze is on the firm – and junior staff are in a vulnerable position. There will be pressures to impress senior staff, to appear adult and to be part of the gang. It is not an easy situation to be in and older Christians can help by their example and moral support.

The work scene is one in which drink may run freely as a matter of course – business lunches can leave people 'well-oiled' when they return to the office – although a surprising number of firms have now restricted or banned the use of drink during working hours. Large organisations should have occupational health departments and a few will have alcohol policies which deal with the way in which people with drink-related problems can be helped.

Whereas school life has a structure which can be influenced and includes planned education, work is totally different. However, personal example is still a powerful way of helping others and Christians may be able to meet together for fellowship and encouragement. Small groups like this can take the initiative and invite the management to let in an outside group to undertake an alcohol education campaign.

7

. . . In leisure time

It has only been during the last twenty years or so that we have come to talk about a 'leisure industry'. Improvements in transport have brought many new facilities within easy reach. Leisure centres are now commonplace. Reduced working hours and longer holidays have given greater opportunity for leisure activities and increasing affluence has enabled more people to participate. Smoking and drinking are regarded as leisure pursuits, either in themselves or as an important accompaniment to something else, and most leisure facilities sell drink and tobacco products.

The English 'pub' is very much part of the leisure scene and one of the most difficult questions to answer reasonably is 'should a Christian go into a pub?' Most pubs have changed out of all recognition. Gone are the bars with spittoons and sawdust! In their place are attractive places which serve good food and provide congenial meeting spots. The 'demon drink' is still there, but a pub does provide more opportunity to control drinking (by refusing to serve people) than does an off-licence or supermarket.

Christians, then, are faced with a problem. If, for many people, a pub provides a 'safe' environment and a place where people meet in a pleasurable atmosphere, should Christians be free to join others there? They will, after all, find many non-Christians there and it could make for golden evangelistic opportunities.

But there are other ways of creating the one-to-one

conversation essential for personal evangelism. Does it necessarily mean going to pubs or clubs? Does it mean hanging around the sports club bar? Does it mean organizing wine and cheese evenings and inviting neighbours? Yet alcohol and tobacco can be very much a part of the social scene and a Christian witness could founder because of negative attitudes and embarrassment. A refusal to go to the pub after work might mean that a chance is lost to build a relationship which might later lead to an opportunity, perhaps elsewhere, to share one's faith.

There are, undoubtedly, situations where Christians should not be seen, and places where one's reputation would be put at risk. If someone is going to put themselves in the way of overwhelming temptation then this should be avoided.

If, however, we feel that going along to the more respectable type of public house is acceptable more questions arise. Does it matter if you actually take an alcoholic drink? Should you accept a cigarette if offered? If you do either, what will that say to the person you are with and for anyone who might see you?

We all have to answer these questions for ourselves, and not only in the context of public houses. Office parties, business lunches and sports club bars all raise these issues. One answer might be to be very careful about the situation in which we are seen drinking or smoking, although this can lead to charges of double standards. Another answer would be to remain drug-free.

If we do not drink in company but enjoy a glass at home, does that make a difference? Some people are acutely aware of their 'example power' and never drink in public. However, it will not be possible to disguise one's habits – people soon find out who drinks or smokes.

There are no absolutely right or wrong answers as to whether Christians should go to pubs. Decisions have to be made according to the situation, although it is possible to develop standard responses which will help. Knowing the different drinks which are available helps, and making sure there is a choice of alcohol-free drinks should be essential. There is much to be said for Christians who can act positively, be seen to be responsible and enjoy themselves.

Leisure time includes hobbies. Home brewing and winemaking are both increasingly popular. These involve making large quantities, particularly with beer. Similar principles apply. Is the drink in your home likely to cause problems for you or your children or guests? If you have large amounts to hand then you may find yourself (and your family) drinking more than you anticipated.

Leisure time can also be used to pass on information and encourage a healthy lifestyle. For example, Radio 1 undertook a 'Rhythm 'n' Booze' campaign to try to get some news about alcohol to young people. Short items of information, jingles and a telephone enquiry all played a part.

As long as preaching is avoided, leisure facilities present an ideal opportunity for positive witness. Churches have used coffee bars and social functions as part of evangelism for years and an increasing number are applying this to alcohol-free bars.

Alcohol-free bars

Seen by some as the successor to coffee bars, it has become fashionable to organise alcohol-free bars and clubs for young people. Christians have taken a lead in setting up many of them. A number of ventures have sprung up around the country and they have included the exotic sounding 'Parrot & Palm Cocktail Club' and Swindon's 'Blind Beggar' pub for young people run by the Salvation Army. Amethyst Centre for Alcohol Concern have produced an excellent book with some case examples (see Appendix 4). However, these ventures already have a chequered history and the original 'Parrot & Palm' club in Worthing has shown how vulnerable it and other youth ventures have been and are to key people moving, as well as the ups and downs of voluntary organisations' cash flow. This can, if one is not careful, lead to the ever-present danger of doing things on the cheap. Alcohol-free drinks then become associated with a shoddy set of surroundings – thus enhancing the image of 'real' drink.

Nevertheless, some ventures have proved very successful in providing safer places for younger people to go and enjoy themselves. The 'Blind Beggar' is in a converted basement and has been well equipped with a pool table, juke-box and bar. It is in the town centre and offers a good place to go in the evening – as well as offering snacks and drinks at lunchtime. This helps make it more of a community facility, just like many pubs. It is run by a manager with support from two full-time staff who are responsible for other activities in the building. The bar takings only pay for one salary and other funds have to be raised to maintain the service. A rota of volunteers provides extra support.

There is no standard pattern and one church in west London adapted the idea for its occasional outreach work. Once or twice a month a bar was opened in their church hall, not unlike a 'traditional' coffee bar. This offered young people a venue with some similarity with the discos and pubs they usually frequent and helped overcome their reluctance to enter a church hall. (Many teenagers have no idea what a church really does and giving them something to relate to is important.)

Running such an activity is not easy, especially if it is open most nights of the week. It requires money, energy and time. It will take great faith and, especially if it is on church premises, understanding and tolerance.

We should beware of leaving it to the inexperienced,

especially if they are also young. Organisational and financial skills are required. Older or more experienced people will be needed to provide support, encouragement, training and, quite possibly, money. But young people with enthusiasm should not be discouraged. They should be given the help which will ultimately enable them to stand on their own feet and give them the character to make decisions. Alcohol-free bars make a positive contribution to reducing alcohol and other drug problems.

Before moving on to consider what can be done within youth work generally and a local church network – where Christians spend much of their leisure time – it is timely to reiterate two of the questions by which a leisure activity can be judged. Does it render you more or less fit for God's service? What effect does your example have on others? God designed us all to enjoy leisure and he gave us a sense of humour, an ability to enjoy physical activity and minds to appreciate art and music. He is interested in us at leisure as well as at work or church.

8

Church youth work

Youth organisations are very concerned about drugs. The YMCA has set up a national drugs project and was responsible for producing a video on drugs starring Lenny Henry (*Chasing the Bandwagon*). British Youth For Christ have sections about drugs in their youth workers' handbook. It would be a very unusual youth organisation, secular or Christian, not to cover drink and other drugs in some way.

Churches and individual Christians are in a unique position to support young people and encourage healthy living. The Christian gospel is about a positive hope. Churches operate in 'leisure time' and can influence young people in the places they choose to attend.

Youth work is not just a matter of opening the doors and seeing who comes in on the night. It requires committed leaders who can relate to young people. Local authorities run long training courses for youth workers and their content shows just how much there is to consider. Steve Chalke's book *The Complete Youth Manual – Volume 1* spends 200 pages on the subject.

The good news is that more emphasis is being placed on training for youth leaders – but even then issues such as alcohol and other drugs may not be covered. Every minister should encourage youth and children's workers to attend training events and ensure they learn about the factors which can destroy or alter young lives. Brainstormers – organised by, among others, British Youth For

Christ – is one event where good training on drugs issues can be had.

Policy matters

Youth leaders need to know where they and their group stand. A 'policy' is a way of stating what you think about something and the ground rules by which you will operate. Considering a 'policy' means thinking about something in advance so as to react positively and rationally. 'Crisis management' yields poor results and usually occurs when leaders have not thought through potential situations before they really happen.

Many youth groups do not have a policy on drugs. For example, what happens if members smoke? What should the leader do if drugs are found? What is the policy on drink? It may be tempting to place these issues to one side because of the need to evangelise or because 'our young people do not have that problem'. That approach is certainly one-sided and probably naive. Policy has to be worked out by carefully considering all the factors. Here are some practical points to consider.

1 '*Evangelism should come before health education*'
Salvation *is* more important than encouraging a young person to be healthy, but an awareness that we all need to be 'born again' does not mean that a blind eye has to be turned to drug use. Young people coming into contact with Christianity need to know that a Christian lifestyle means God's salvation touching every part of us, being fit for God's service and showing a positive example to others. Ignoring drug use compromises the Christian message and presents at best a defective model of discipleship and at worst an encouragement to experiment with drugs. If potential Christians view the 'discipline' of a church youth group as being lax then this will become part of their view of the Christian life and do more harm than good. Evangelism and Christian discipleship are

inseparably linked. We aim not to make converts but disciples, and this means that the whole gospel must be presented and clear standards set from the start.

2 *Setting rules*

Young people will accept rules rather more readily when they are given explanations than when they are simply told to do something. Smoking is almost universally accepted as being dangerous to health and, in addition, is a fire risk! Illegal drug use is against the law, and young people know that risks are involved even if they think the benefits outweigh the costs – or that they will never succumb to a problem. Youth leaders have this existing evidence of harm that can be used when explaining their reasons for the church policy on drugs. A ban on alcohol can be defended on legal grounds as well as explaining about the health and social risks.

Rules for a youth group should not be made up as you go along and, in addition, they should be considered in the light of church policy. They should be worked out carefully, in the light of biblical principles and with prayer.

3 *Smoking*

Rules do not stop people smoking, but they do provide a framework within which to control things. Smoking causes problems in a number of ways.

1 The health risk to the smokers and those in their company (through 'passive smoking').
2 Peer pressure to smoke being exerted on other members.
3 Litter outside the entrances.
4 Older church members feeling intimidated by youths standing outside and looking tough.
5 Fire risk.
6 People leaving meetings for ten minutes at a time to have a smoke.

Some of these problems are universal – they arise whenever people smoke. Some are particular to smoking by young people on church premises. Every youth leader needs to identify their own problems. But before tackling any of these problems the leadership has to be aware of two important factors. First, smoking is addictive and few people find it easy to give up. For most it will be a long, hard struggle. Second, if any of the leaders smoke, action will be made even more difficult.

The health risk can be dealt with by giving information. There are many good leaflets and posters available. If there are members of the group who are non-smokers and who are obviously fit and healthy then this will reinforce the message. Harnessing a positive role for this group will also help reverse the peer pressure which often encourages smoking. Non-smokers should be encouraged and their attitudes will be reinforced by this. A new factor is emerging with the increasing evidence that passive smoking (simply being in the company of those who are smoking) can be damaging to health.

Litter may seem a trivial point but it can breed ill-will. Young people will need to be reminded not to leave their matches and cigarette ends about, but it could be counter-productive to place a bin outside the door because that might legitimise the smoking!

'Intimidation' is a real problem if older people have to walk by a 'gang' of youths, however harmless they may be. This sort of problem may occur on Sunday nights while young people hang around for an after-church meeting. Like litter, this is something that should be solved by good humour and encouragement rather than pushing the 'offenders' twenty yards down the road.

The fire risk is a tried and trusted method of banning smoking, particularly if some of the leaders smoke but you want to stop it on the premises. The difficulty is that it fails to deal with the real issue and can often look like – and be – an easy way out for those who want to avoid confrontation or discussion.

Regular smokers do have the urge to walk out for five

or ten minutes because they need a 'quick drag'. That does disrupt proceedings. Leaders should set their ground rules from the start and firmly explain that it is disruptive to have people wandering in and out. It will be best to set this in the context of the difficulty it creates for the whole group, not just the leaders. A well-handled group discussion in which various members are encouraged to share their feelings might be one way of dealing with this.

We had some of these problems at our own church and, after discussion at a leader's meeting, re-affirmed our view that smoking was dangerous to health and also unpleasant. We decided that youth events should continue to be 'no smoking' occasions and that smoking just outside the premises should be discouraged. We recognised the impossibility of stopping young people from smoking unless they made their own decisions to quit, but we did allocate time to explain our policy, using both health evidence and biblical principles for healthy living. Besides confirming the position (which does have to be done now and again because of new members arriving and failing memories) it also gave an opportunity for the non-smokers to encourage their smoking friends to stop, or at least desist in their presence. Enforcement on outside activities is difficult and relies on the good humour of the leaders to be persuasive enough to stop the smoking.

4 *Drinking*

Alcoholic drink raises issues similar to those which arise with smoking, although action is more difficult because there is often no understanding that drinking can be harmful. Such ignorance is as prevalent amongst leaders as young people! Drinking has the sort of image which smoking used to have and many of the approaches outlined for dealing with smoking could be used.

If pub-going and under-age drinking is a problem then a subtle adjustment to a youth group's opening hours might help. There would be no need to go right up to pub closing time . . . finishing a few minutes beforehand would still make it difficult to get a drink!

5 *Legal problems*

What should a youth leader do if a group member is spotted buying cigarettes when under sixteen (or drinks if under eighteen) or is discovered with an illegal drug? There are a number of options available. Speaking to the young person or the seller, approaching the parents or going to the police are just three of them. It might even be that a young person confesses to the use of an illegal drug and says who supplied it, etc. Should a leader warn the individual, report the supplier or do nothing?

The worst decision would be to ignore the situation in the hope that it will go away. That solves nothing. Speaking to the person concerned would be a good start because that gives them a chance to tell their side of the story. Nothing is ever simple and they might, for example, have been buying cigarettes for a visiting relative. Such a discussion gives an opportunity to assess whether any further action needs to be taken. The aim should always be to help the individuals concerned to think about their actions and move towards change as appropriate.

If further action is needed make sure the young person knows what is to be done. In some circumstances, it may be necessary to remove an individual from membership. This should always be a last resort, but in the case of powerful individuals setting negative examples there may be no alternative.

In the case of illegal drugs, telling parents or the police should not be ruled out, particularly if the young people show every sign of continuing to obtain drugs. If they cannot stop themselves then others will need to be involved.

6 *Holidays and retreats*
Taking young people away from their familiar environment brings formal and informal opportunities for teaching and encouragement. The former relates to the programme and the main purpose – be it holiday or study. The latter concerns the type of atmosphere that could be fostered and is more concerned with lifestyle. A social activity could include refreshments and alcohol-free drinks to give them a taste for alternatives and practice in choosing them.

Personal example is a potent force which leaders should not underestimate while away from home. Young people inevitably inspect adult behaviour and they will copy anything that is attractive. Leaders' attitudes to drugs are only one of many things that will emerge during the time a youth group lives together.

Christian youth work is a vital area when it comes to the promotion of healthy drug-free living. Teenagers, especially the younger ones, are forming life-long habits and there is potential to encourage them to think about their options and not just follow the crowd. Youth workers should remember that the informal times shape these attitudes as it is then that young people choose for themselves. Formal teaching is important, but if the surrounding activities and the examples of leaders and other older Christians does not reinforce it, then it will be wasted.

9

The local church

Local churches come in all shapes and sizes and for this chapter's purpose can be defined as any worshipping group of Christians. What might a church do in its local community about drink and other drug abuse?

Leadership

Leaders, whatever their personal position on consuming alcohol or using tobacco, should be prepared to give advice about all drugs. Paul tells the church leaders in Ephesus to care for the flock (Acts 20: 28). Amongst other things this means that the teaching programme should relate biblical principles to Christian living, and from time to time will touch on the question of drugs. In pastoral ministry there will be a need to understand the people who come for help with a drug problem.

This means that church leaders should be given opportunities to learn about alcohol and other drugs. Training colleges need to equip people with the basic facts, to remove the myths which were mentioned earlier and to make sure that people know where to find help (if they cannot offer support themselves). There also need to be opportunities for in-service training for church workers. (Information and courses are available from a number of agencies listed in Appendix 2).

All churches have some form of voluntary leadership. Youth leaders and Sunday school teachers, leaders of women's groups, Brigade officers, small group leaders and many others will benefit from some form of training. Churches should ensure that at least one or two leaders are given the responsibility to find out what alcohol and other drug education is available and where help can be sought.

Alcohol-free or responsible drinking?

Different denominations have taken different views about alcohol, and many of the Free churches played a large part in the temperance movement of the last century. Many more Christians now drink, but the historical positions of the different churches can still cause division and misunderstanding between those who drink and those who do not.

For example, Methodism has never adopted a compulsory total abstinence stance and, in fact, early Methodists were not usually total abstainers. It was not until the mid-nineteenth century that the denomination began, with the growth of the Band of Hope and other organisations in the temperance movement, to swing towards total abstinence. The modern Methodist response to drink is to accept that total abstinence is a worthwhile objective while agreeing that responsible drinking is also acceptable for Christians. Indeed, it is difficult to envisage any other position being adopted given that, like other denominations, Methodists have their teetotallers and their 'responsible drinkers'!

The history of our churches is marred by divisions over alcohol. But drinking and non-drinking Christians should build bridges rather than barriers. There is more than enough for Christians to do together in attempting to reduce the level of drink-related harm in Britain. To be effective, bridge-building has to take place within a local church and all Christians, regardless of their drinking habits, should try to periodically examine their position and try to understand why others take a different view.

Policy

Given the huge scale of drug-related problems today, all churches should consider their policy about drink, tobacco or any other drugs. In practice, alcoholic drinks will need greater attention because most Christians do not smoke or take other drugs. However, a policy about tobacco may be needed, if only to state whether smoking is allowed on or near the premises.

One area where there should be a clear policy is that of drink on the premises. Should wedding receptions held in church halls be allowed to serve champagne for toasts? Should other events be permitted to take place with alcoholic refreshment? The Churches Council On Alcohol and Drugs published a leaflet (*Alcohol on the Premises?*) which set out some facts and examples for churches to consider. Three examples were used to illustrate the factors involved in coming to a decision about alcohol on the premises. These examples offer an opportunity to learn from others who have already faced up to the issue and they are reprinted below. (They do cover some of the ground which was discussed in earlier chapters, but are reproduced in full because they show how those involved worked their views out.)

1 *A Baptist church*

In the autumn of 1985 the pastors and deacons of Thornhill Baptist Church, Southampton, decided to review their church's position on alcohol. They drafted a Reaffirmation of Church Policy as a basis for their discussions. This led to a further paper, which sought to clarify some of the issues, before a final statement was circulated to the church through their magazine. That paper read:

Guidelines regarding alcohol and church functions – a statement by the pastors and deacons.

For many years our church has operated a 'no alcohol' rule on its premises. We have done this as our corporate witness against alcohol abuse in society.

Since this rule was established, Christian attitudes to alcohol have changed and it is now harder to maintain a united witness on this issue. Within our fellowship there are genuine differences between those who practise total abstention and those who drink in moderation. We acknowledge this division and accept that this must remain a matter of individual conscience. However despite this tension it is important that we make a stand on this issue as a fellowship.

As a leadership we are concerned at the growing problem of alcohol abuse in our country, particularly amongst young people. We are also concerned at the way this problem is affecting individuals within our fellowship.

In the present atmosphere therefore we feel it is important to reaffirm our commitment to the stand which we have made as a church over the years. We endorse the 'no alcohol' rule on our church premises. In order to be consistent in our witness we feel that the 'spirit' of this rule should also apply to any church function held off the premises. In other words, if the church or a church group is organising a fellowship activity for the church, no alcohol should be provided.

We have shared this matter with the house group leaders and youth leaders and they support us in this interpretation of church policy. We hope that you will understand and support us too. Respecting each other's viewpoint, may we as a fellowship have a united concern and maintain a positive witness against the growing social evil of alcohol abuse?

A similar statement was presented to a youth leaders' meeting just prior to the publication of the final statement. It read:

Guidelines regarding alcohol and church and youth functions.

During our last meeting 'drink' was mentioned as one of the problems that concern us, as youth leaders, among young people. This concern has also been felt by the church leadership as a whole.

. . . However, despite this tension [the differences of views] it is still important that we make a stand on this issue, especially as those working among young people where the problem of alcohol abuse is growing fast . . .

. . . In addition . . . we as youth leaders recognise that we have an added responsibility in this area to present a wholesome example to the young people in our care: in our actions, words and attitudes towards alcohol.

Therefore, respecting each other's viewpoint, we strive to maintain a united concern and positive witness against the growing social evil of alcohol abuse.

2 *A Quaker meeting*

Members of the Milton Keynes Meeting of the Religious Society of Friends (Quakers) held two lengthy meetings early in 1986. The first took nearly an hour on the agenda of a monthly business meeting. After a fortnight a second, well-attended gathering devoted two hours to this particular concern, and produced the following Minute:

Meeting held on 16 March, 1986. Minute 7. Alcohol on the premises.

We are aware of the personal, social and economic consequences of the misuse of alcohol and the problems associated with it. We accept our individual and corporate responsibility to show by example that alcohol is not necessary for enjoyment and good fellowship. We agree that alcohol shall not be brought into, or consumed upon, our premises as a general rule.

On any specific occasion when the serving of alcohol

is requested, permission must be obtained from the appropriate body, who will consider each application individually. It will be understood that at such functions a sufficient range of alternative drinks will be provided. If other rooms are available for use, we would prefer drinks to be served elsewhere than in the main meeting room.

We agree that the Marriage Guidance Council, as daily users, with us, of the centre, should not be covered by this restriction. Our clerk is asked to forward to them a copy of this Minute so that they may understand our position.

3 *A West Midlands Anglican church*

This church, medium-sized, in the town centre, has a long tradition of not serving alcohol at church functions. On a once-off basis, the Parish Church Council (PCC) gave permission for alcoholic drink to be served at two social occasions which were organised as part of an evangelistic weekend. Subsequently the PCC discussed whether the arrangement should be continued on future occasions or whether the church should revert to its previous 'non-alcoholic' tradition.

The following paper was offered to the PCC by a church member as one contribution to its discussions in April 1985.

1 *Biblical attitudes to alcohol*

In general, the consumption of alcohol is not forbidden in either the Old or New Testaments. In Old Testament times wine was in use, usually diluted one part wine to three parts water. Spirits were not available. In New Testament times the Jews used wine both at home and in the synagogue in a reverent manner on solemn occasions. Our Lord provided and used wine. Paul too used wine and recommended its medical use to Timothy, but also commended abstinence in certain circumstances. Drunkenness is condemned throughout the Bible, as is the abuse of the body generally.

2 *Some biblical principles relevant to decision making*
It is inappropriate to decide on a course of action which may cause another Christian to damage himself, even though the course of action may be sound in itself and perfectly satisfactory for the majority. It may be necessary to go beyond normal limits ('the second mile') to safeguard some of the people around us. Any decision must take account of the need to have compassion on anyone who is suffering.

3 *The alcohol problem in Britain*
Currently, Britain has a very serious alcohol problem. This problem is described in detail in a 1979 report, entitled *Alcohol and Alcoholism*, prepared by a committee of the Royal College of Psychiatrists (the professional body for doctors practising in the field of nervous and mental disorders).

The following are a few quotations from the report:

'Consumption per head of the population and damage to health caused by alcohol are closely associated, though in ways that are poorly understood. In the light of this, the increase of annual per capita consumption of alcohol in the UK between 1950 and 1976 from 5.2 litres to 9.7 litres gives cause for grave concern.

'The evidence is not only that a problem of great size exists, but one which in nearly every aspect is on an upward climb.

'What is fundamentally at stake: lives are being ruined on a large scale by the abuse of alcohol. It is necessary to look beyond the statistics to the personal realities of suffering, wasted lives and family misery.

'Society should, though, be appalled at the present state of affairs and entirely unwilling to witness continued loss and suffering of this unnecessary order [of magnitude].

'We believe that an undoubted message for the future is that prevention has to be strengthened, and that this will inevitably mean all of us drinking somewhat less.

'Only the sum of a great many small and symbolic actions within the community will slowly alter attitudes that have to be altered.'

Some recommendations from the report for strengthening the prevention of alcohol abuse are as follows:

'Anyone driving a vehicle should not drink at all before driving.

'A review should be made in every community of the extent to which leisure activities are available (particularly for the young) that do not engender pressures to drink. Appropriate action should be taken to increase the range of such activities.

'There should be a commitment to preventing the national per capita consumption from rising beyond the present level.

'. . . some agreement should be reached as to the level to which alcohol consumption and indices of harm should be brought down over the next decade.'

The report describes the state of affairs which existed in 1978. The same adverse trends have continued since then and are described in a report in *Which* for October 1984.

4 *Some reasons for serving alcohol at church functions*

It reduces apprehension on the part of visitors coming into strange surroundings.

It helps create a relaxed and social atmosphere.

Many people expect alcohol to be served on social occasions.

Some people consider that it is inconsistent for alcohol to be served in the homes of church members but not at church functions.

5 *Some consequences of serving alcohol at church functions*

The social use of alcohol to produce some measure of relaxation also produces some reduction of self-control. Since self-control is one of the fruits of the Spirit specifically mentioned in the Bible, a possible consequence is a dishonouring of the Spirit. The use of alcohol to reduce apprehension involves the risk of encouraging alcohol dependence. The serving of alcohol at church functions may be regarded as a 'seal of approval', thus putting quite severe pressure on some who do not at present use it. It will make church functions unattractive for those who do not use alcohol.

It will constitute an increase in alcohol consumption at a time when many responsible secular authorities are appealing for a reduction. In so doing, it will ignore the suffering of the increasing number of people harmed by alcohol.

6 *Some reasons for not serving alcohol at church functions*

It will be a demonstration of the power of the Holy Spirit, working through prayerful, hard working, caring and compassionate Christians, to provide happy and enjoyable social occasions without the use of alcohol.

It is no longer enough to use alcohol 'wisely' or 'moderately'. A positive demonstration of love and concern is needed for those already suffering in any way from the effects of alcohol.

It will show a readiness to stand alongside those from the secular world who have given a lead and are prepared to take some action, however small, to reduce the abuse of alcohol. Christians should not lag behind in response to a call to alleviate and prevent suffering.

It shows compassion for those who should not drink any alcohol – alcoholics under treatment or 'cured' (total abstinence is still the preferred, though not the only treatment for alcoholics), those who are under the doctor's orders not to take alcohol (eg pregnant women, those suffering from some stomach or liver complaints) and those who will be driving home.

7 Conclusion
The biblical principles concerning the responsibilities of Christians to other men and women, both inside and outside the faith, together with the serious alcohol problem in the nation generally, seem to point strongly in the direction of a 'no alcohol' policy for church functions, particularly when account is taken of the previous tradition of our church.

In October 1985 the PCC decided not to have alcohol at church functions; the European Cup Final riot at the Heysel Stadium in Brussels was one factor contributing to the withdrawal of a proposal to use alcohol on an occasional basis. In 1986 the practice was that only non-alcoholic drinks were served – usually a fruit cup.

All these fellowships must have had one thing in common – members who drank alcohol – and yet they all decided that the issue of drink was serious enough for them to make a corporate statement. All their members accepted that they could set a positive example that would be effective despite personal differences.

Holy Communion

The celebration of Communion, by whatever name it is known, is another area where attitudes differ. A substantial number of churches, mainly non-conformist, will use an alcohol-free liquid to represent the wine – some using grape juice and others something like Ribena.

Where alcoholic wine is used the small amount of alcohol consumed will be harmless for most people but there are other factors a church should consider. Those using alcoholic wine will say that they are being true to Bible times and that there are sufficient scriptural references about the joyous nature of wine to make this a reasonable choice. In addition, there is the feeling that the antiseptic nature of alcohol kills any germs when one chalice is used for the whole congregation. There is also a strong sense of tradition which surrounds the use of wine.

Those taking the other view reflect some of the unease felt in using a substance related to so much human suffering, as well as appreciating that non-alcoholic grape juices were also consumed in Bible times. In addition, some people cannot take any alcohol for health reasons, and alcoholics often say that only a few drops would be enough to start them drinking heavily again. Using a non-alcoholic grape juice enables everyone to take part.

In some churches, the priest is required to consume all the unused drink. This can be a great burden for those clergy who have an alcohol problem. A few years ago news came from the United States that some Roman Catholic priests had been given a special dispensation because consuming the remaining wine made their alcohol problems much worse.

Except for tradition, it is difficult to see why a church has to use alcoholic wine. Scripture refers to the 'cup' which Jesus passed around at the Last Supper, and it is what it symbolises that is important.

Social responsibility

It has become fashionable for churches to set up social responsibility groups. Such groups could well discuss alcohol and drug-related matters. For example, a church may be concerned about the number of pubs, clubs and other licensed premises nearby, especially if there is an under-age drinking problem. Opposing licence applications is reasonably straightforward and could be discussed in a social responsibility committee. In Kingswood, Bristol, the local Christian Council opposed a garage's application for a licence – and enlisted the support of their borough council. They 'won', and made a positive contribution to their witness by working with the elected authority.

Opposing a licence application can appear to be a daunting prospect, but in reality magistrates' courts operate according to set rules and will often encourage an inexperienced 'opposer' to receive a fair hearing. Ordinary people can object at this level and a well prepared case will often win the day.

In the event of a Parliamentary debate on a drug-related issue, a social responsibility committee or its equivalent could formulate a response for discussion and approval by the whole church. They can be a useful means of disseminating information through special meetings, displays or leaflets. They can organise special prayer meetings or keep drug-related issues on the regular prayer agenda for the church.

If a church is going to use a social responsibility committee as a means of making its Christian opinion known in the secular world, then it does have to ensure that decisions can be made and acted on fairly quickly. The Licensing Bill which went through Parliament in 1987/8 had its second reading quite soon after being introduced and this left many people unable to respond because they could not work through their system quickly enough.

But not everything depends on committees! Individuals can press for change, too. For example, the Government seems to pay more attention to illegal drug abuse and this could be the starting point for correspondence with your MP urging that more resources be put towards the greater problems related to alcohol. Members of Parliament are sensitive to constituent's views. If you do write to your MP, try to ask him or her to do something or to express an opinion. This technique will mean that you can open a dialogue rather than receive a short letter 'noting your views'.

A letter on alcohol problems need not always be general: there are specific policy changes for which you can ask. For example, if you feel that the legal alcohol level in drivers' blood should be reduced then make your voice heard. If you favour random breath testing, write in and say so! In 1988 the Government chose six areas in which to try out a ban on drinking in public places – the most publicised being the city centre of Coventry. It was felt that this would reduce threatening behaviour. If you want something similar for your town centre then you need to lobby your local council, write to your MP and send a press release to all local newspapers encouraging others to join in the campaign.

Then there is the matter of health education. Government funded services like the NHS have local bodies who should be asked to do something. There will be a local Health Promotion Department (write to the General Manager) and the local Family Health Services Authority organises General Medical Practitioner, Dental and Pharmaceutical services (write to the General Manager). A group called the Community Health Council is supposed to represent consumer interests – that is you and me! Again: write and make your views known.

Another area for Christian involvement is in attempting to reduce the exaggerations and glossy pictures of life presented in advertisements. The Advertising Standards Authority and Independent Broadcasting Association operate codes of practice with which advertisers should comply. For example, nobody under the age of twenty-five should appear in drink advertisements and there should be no link with sex or sport.

Prayer

It only costs time, but to pray knowledgeably requires taking some trouble to find out local and other needs and then to introduce them to the congregation. There is plenty to pray about where drink and other drugs are concerned. You could spend some time praying for young people you know – who will meet peer pressure and opportunities to fall foul of legal (and illegal) drugs as they grow older. Or, perhaps, you could pray for the work of Christian rehabilitation and education agencies.

With so many prayer diaries and letters flying around the Christian community, it is actually quite difficult to introduce new needs. It needs one or more individuals to be committed to find out more and then acquaint others of the facts involved. Alcohol and other drug issues have no particular claim to be more important prayer topics than missionary work or evangelism, but they have tended to have a lower profile and need more exposure.

Giving

Drink and drug problems are generally acknowledged to be serious and there is widespread acceptance that 'something has to be done'. That makes it all the more important for Christians to examine their financial response.

All the Christian organisations involved in dealing with drug problems are small and do not have the funds to mount big advertising campaigns. They rely on churches and Christians to identify them as worthy causes. Who has heard of the Coke Hole Trust in Hampshire or Yeldall Manor near Reading? How many people know that the Band of Hope cannot meet all its opportunities to provide Christian-based health education because of lack of funds, or that Christian rehabilitation agencies exist on shoe-string budgets with their staff working under great pressure?

These organisations do not have the time to publicise their own activities and their staff are more suited to caring and educational work than selling themselves. Part of the reason for creating the Evangelical Coalition on Drugs was to make churches aware that such organisations exist and can provide a service, but they need the wherewithal to do so. Giving is one way of supporting

Christian organisations involved and a first step could be to find out if your church has any local groups which need support.

Helping people with problems

Helping people who have problems with the abuse of alcohol and other drugs is a big subject, and is dealt with more fully in the following chapter. Some aspects which relate particularly to local church work are presented here.

A few churches have linked themselves with organisations which offer help. Some churches have set up a service for themselves. An example of the latter is the Kaleidoscope Drugs Project set up by Kingston Baptist Church in London, which features in Appendix 7. Such involvement calls for a lot of commitment and a real calling to service. If you want to do this then take a visit to one or more of the organisations concerned and ask lots of questions.

There are other ways to care for those with addiction problems. Youth workers need counselling skills which include an ability to help, or at least understand, a drug user. Often that help will be to direct the drug user to a professional agency. Thc practical section at the end of the book contains suggestions about how to find out who provides services in your locality. It is important to understand what is available. There is a danger of simply duplicating existing facilities with something that has a Christian flavour. This is usually unnecessary. For example, a church could use a 'secular' service such as a Council on Alcoholism or a drugs project and introduce a Christian element by making someone welcome outside of their visits to a drugs counsellor.

Churches and individuals must beware of 'preaching' and always be ready to seek advice and help themselves. It is not enough to say, 'Jesus will set you free.' He can, of course, but it requires much more than words. Counselling may be a long-term commitment and involves accepting a person as they are – inevitably with their feelings of inadequacy, rejection, inferiority and a lack of love. And do remember that introducing drug users to a church service can be a traumatic experience: meeting with a house group or gathering of Christian friends is a beneficial and more gentle introduction to God's people.

Talking to a number of staff from different organisations, they would welcome local churches contacting them and offering to provide some form of support for those people who are ready to attempt normal life again. Think about that as you read the next chapter and learn something of their work.

An appropriate Christian response to the problems of alcohol and other drugs is something which every church needs to work out. That means developing a coherent, biblical policy; thinking about (and doing!) something to press local and national decision makers for beneficial changes; supporting relevant Christian agencies: caring for those in need.

10

Helping people with problems

Care and cure

In the case of a broken leg or a common cold we know what sort of care is appropriate and what results to expect. Dealing with drug problems is much more complex. Because people are all different, a range of treatment and counselling methods are necessary. There is no one standard response which applies to all drug users. This is not always understood and there are those, for example, who are convinced that the only way for alcoholics or drug addicts to control their addiction is to follow the twelve steps of Alcoholics Anonymous. Others place more emphasis on the situation which individuals find themselves in and adopt a 'behavioural approach'.

And how long will it take to cure the problem? We can all see that care is necessary while somebody is trying to come off a drug and is suffering the after effects – called 'withdrawal'. It is harder to understand that care should not stop with physical withdrawal. Drug addicts have a tendency to return to their habits and caring must continue even when they appear to have completely recovered. Addicts have a natural tendency to feel that the drug can be handled the next time around and so they may fail to make adequate safeguards. Old friends appear and are very persuasive. The pressures of life are tough for a recovered addict because it is difficult to find employment and there may be ongoing health or psychiatric problems.

As well as the ever present danger of a relapse, addicts may suffer permanent mental or physical damage from drug abuse. For example, alcoholics, even when recovered, sometimes show a tendency to be forgetful and less than reliable. Smokers, even when they have stopped, have to live with the damage they have done to their bodies.

All these factors mean that working with drug misusers is a hard and emotionally demanding job, especially for those who run residential facilities where they cannot 'escape' from their clients. Many who misuse drugs have deprived emotional backgrounds – a lack of 'tender loving care' – and any rehabilitation work has to re-establish this emotional component. Simply drying someone out does not solve their problems.

The complexity and long-term nature of caring properly for drug abusers means that Christians need to be aware of the wide range of services available. These include. . .

1 *Health and social services*

Although a large number of different organisations are concerned with drug use, the main brunt of providing help falls on the health and social services. The courts, prison and probation services are also involved as so many people commit crimes whilst under the influence of alcohol or other drugs.

Within the National Health Service, the first line of approach is often the General Practitioner. They are the doorway into most parts of the system as they refer patients to hospitals or to specialised drug or alcohol clinics. Some people with drink or drug problems, however, may not want to go to somebody who has a longstanding relationship with their family, and so specialised clinics will take self-referrals – people who come directly to them without the knowledge of their GP.

Patients who are to receive treatment for alcohol and drug dependence problems are often admitted to psychiatric hospitals. But a significant proportion of admissions to medical wards in general hospitals are for conditions – especially accidents or physical damage – which have drink or drugs as a related factor. In some places this can be as high as one in five.

HIV/AIDS is a special case. The care of AIDS sufferers is a drug-related issue because HIV can be transmitted by the use of dirty needles. In addition, those under the influence of a drug may also neglect to use contraceptives and so spread AIDS through promiscuous sexual activity. Christians have been in the forefront of initiatives to care for AIDS sufferers – the Mildmay Mission Hospital in east London is a case in point.

2 *Self-help groups*

Alcoholics Anonymous is perhaps the best known of the organisations which helps groups of addicts support themselves by meeting together and sharing problems. It has two related organisations, called Al-Anon and Al-A-Teen, because the families of alcoholics also need support. Al-Anon is for spouses and Al-A-Teen for children of alcoholics. All work on the same principle of meeting together as a group on a regular basis. The programme of Alcoholics Anonymous is built on their twelve traditions, the short form of which is reproduced below.

1 Our common welfare should come first; personal recovery depends upon AA unity.
2 For our group purpose there is but one ultimate authority – a loving God as he may express himself in our group conscience. Our leaders are but trusted servants; they do not govern.
3 The only requirement for AA membership is a desire to stop drinking.

4 Each group should be autonomous except in matters affecting other groups or AA as a whole.
5 Each group has but one primary purpose – to carry its message to the alcoholic who still suffers.
6 An AA group ought never endorse, finance or lend the AA name to any related facility or outside enterprise, lest problems of money, property and prestige divert us from our primary purpose.
7 Every AA group ought to be fully self-supporting, declining outside contributions.
8 Alcoholics Anonymous should remain forever non-professional, but our service centres may employ special workers.
9 AA, as such, ought never be organised; but we may create service boards or committees directly responsible to those they serve.
10 Alcoholics Anonymous has no opinion on outside issues; hence the AA name ought never be drawn into public controversy.
11 Our public relations policy is based on attraction rather than promotion; we need always to maintain personal anonymity at the level of press, radio and films.
12 Anonymity is the spiritual foundation of our traditions, ever reminding us to place principles before personalities.

For anyone wanting to find out more about Alcoholics Anonymous, their number is always in telephone directories. As a guide to finding out whether anyone has a problem with their drinking, Alcoholics Anonymous have prepared twelve questions, and if someone answers Yes to any one of them then they should look seriously at their habit and seek help. The questions are as follows:

1 Do you drink because you have problems? To face up to stressful situations?

2 Do you drink when you get mad at other people, your friends or parents?

3 Do you often prefer to drink alone, rather than with others?

4 Are you starting to get low marks? Are you skiving off work?

5 Do you ever try to stop or drink less – and fail?

6 Have you begun to drink in the morning, before school or work?

7 Do you gulp your drinks as if to satisfy a great thirst?

8 Do you ever have loss of memory due to your drinking?

9 Do you avoid being honest with others about your drinking?

10 Do you ever get into trouble when you are drinking?

11 Do you often get drunk when you drink, even when you do not mean to?

12 Do you think you're big to be able to hold your drink?

(The Twelve Questions, from *Too Young*, are reprinted with the permission of AA World Services, Inc.)

Alcoholics Anonymous, Al-Anon and Al-A-Teen are group organisations and there can be wide variations in the character of each local meeting. Some, undeniably, take the Christian God as the higher power who can offer salvation through Jesus Christ. Others use the concept of a higher power as something to cling to but there is no sense of a loving God who gives victory in Christ. If one is looking for a Christian group to support an alcoholic then it would be sensible to find out what sort of attitude the local Alcoholics Anonymous group takes before making an unqualified recommendation. Remember, though, that their type of meeting will reflect the attitudes of existing members and it is possible for a group's character to change slowly as new people arrive and old ones leave.

Group meetings for addicts are not confined to Alcoholics Anonymous and Narcotics Anonymous. One Christian group which works with alcoholics in a similar way is the Stauros Foundation, which places a strong emphasis on the Christian message of salvation through Jesus. They link their groups with a worker who supports the alcoholics.

3 *Community based work*

Day centres were the most common provision for drug users in the early 1970s but now only a few remain. In addition, there are a number of projects run by groups like Turning Point (a voluntary organisation which co-ordinates drug abuse and alcoholism projects). These facilities will offer a range of activities such as workshops, individual counselling, group work and assistance with difficulties like homelessness and legal and social security problems. Other projects have workers who go out into a locality from a central base.

Information on what is available locally should be obtainable from one of the Councils of Alcoholism that have become well-established throughout Britain. Although such councils now have a range of different titles, such as Alcohol Counselling or Advisory Services, they all offer information and advice. In addition, drug advisory centres exist in a number of areas and these groups usually include alcohol with the other drugs. Their telephone numbers will be in local directories or available from a Citizens Advice Bureau.

4 *Residential work*

Hospitals and social service hostels provide the basic care within the welfare services. Half-way houses provide a safe environment while someone is in the transitional phase from being an addict to taking up life in the community again. Therapeutic communities offer long-term residential support.

Other establishments are based on what has been described as the 'Minnesota' model – a pattern originating in Minnesota, USA. These places have a similar approach to Alcoholics Anonymous in that they see alcoholism and drug addiction as a disease which affects certain individuals. They offer short-term residential care, often on a medical basis with nurses and doctors. In Britain the 'Minnesota' model is the preserve of private health care establishments which may offer some assisted places for those who cannot pay. They will regard addiction as a chronic and incurable illness and one such unit set its goals for treatment as:

1 total abstinence and its support and maintenance,
2 the development of an improved lifestyle.

They try to focus on those areas of a person's life which may act as immediate triggers to further drug usage and those factors which stimulate and maintain addiction. Their treatment approach is short, intensive and structured and, because they feel that lengthy residential care can be disabling, they aim to return the patient to community life as rapidly as possible.

They use the philosophy of the Alcoholics Anonymous programme and, where possible, they employ counsellors who are themselves recovered alcohol or drug dependent persons. A doctor usually retains overall responsibility for the care of the patients. Treatment is shared by a team of other professionals including nurses and counsellors.

They do take people who are still under the influence of drugs and, during the initial period, patients will be under close nursing supervision. Group therapy is conducted by a trained counsellor. Lectures cover the physical effects of alcohol and drug abuse and patients attend meetings of Alcoholics Anonymous and Narcotics Anonymous during their stay. Family involvement in treatment is considered essential.

A spiritual element may exist with opportunities for

patients to attend services and perhaps go out to churches in the locality.

Some Christian therapeutic communities take smaller groups of people for much longer periods than is typical of the 'Minnesota' model. Their funding comes from social security 'board and lodging' allowances, gifts and fund raising rather than private payments. Although a willingness to accept Christianity is not a pre-condition of entry, these groups feel that coming off drugs has to be tied in with Christian growth for a long-term answer.

Yeldall Manor is fairly typical of such therapeutic communities. It is part of the Yeldall Christian Centre group and is a large country house, set in its own grounds, near Reading. Seeing the need to work within a community as well as providing a residential facility 'away from the crowd', the organisation has three houses in Hounslow linked to the work at Yeldall Manor.

Yeldall Manor recognises that, in order to effect rehabilitation, they need to deal with the 'complete person' and this must include a spiritual dimension. Their statement of belief begins by accepting the Bible as the 'inspired, infallible and authoritative Word of God'. Their membership of the Evangelical Alliance has led to a key involvement in the Evangelical Coalition on Drugs.

They opened their doors to up to twenty drug dependent men in 1977 and their referral guide sees 'love and discipline as the major means of change' in the life of a resident. The guide speaks of. . . .

Love – 'through Christ's love we seek to provide an emotionally secure and supportive environment in which real change can take place. Open, honest, trusting and caring relationships are seen as essential if a resident is to have the security to be himself, to let his "image" slip. For this reason we seek to practise such relationships in the knowledge that the residents then have the freedom to become open, honest, trusting and caring individuals.'

Discipline – 'given the resident's previous chaotic antisocial lifestyle and/or his inability to apply self-discipline to even the most reasonable of social behavioural patterns, we see discipline as necessary to bring about true freedom from himself.'

Three major factors are considered when assessing an applicant's suitability for acceptance at Yeldall.

1 Is there a genuine motivation for change?
2 Are there positive professional references supporting the person?
3 Will the applicant be compatible with the staff and residents?

Residents have to sign an agreement which places certain constraints on behaviour. They are not allowed, for example, to:

1 Become involved in the occult.
2 Wear jewellery relating to previous lifestyles.
3 Enter a new relationship with a woman until they are well on the road to recovery.
4 Bring in any records or tapes.
5 Smoke indoors or during the working hours.

The agreement also sets out the proposition that real change will be in direct proportion to:

1 Willingness to use every aspect of the programme positively and consistently.
2 Willingness to be open and realistic about every aspect of life to themselves, their team leader and other staff;
3 Willingness to share with the team leader whenever they break the contract – including those times away from Yeldall Manor.

This agreement seeks to ensure that nobody is under any false illusions on arrival. Rehabilitation is not easy, especially when it is seen as involving a holistic approach, rather than a simplistic 'drying out'.

The long-term approach of Yeldall Manor is in

marked contrast to the shorter term treatment offered by the 'Minnesota' model. Both types of programme seem to work for some and this is another indication that different treatment programmes suit different people.

However, although there are different types of residential care, the provision of facilities is constantly changing. Centres may cease to operate (because they have insufficient funds) or change their rationale quite markedly. The drug rehabilitation world has not found a stability of its own, and it will always be wise to check current policies rather than relying on old information. The Band of Hope has produced a directory of Christian based caring agencies in this field.

In recent years there has been a growing interest in 'harm reduction', which is an approach which accepts that users can reduce their consumption and perhaps stabilise at a lower level of use – or transfer to a less harmful substance. This does not fit easily with rehabilitation programmes which seek to remove completely the need to use drugs. Appendix 7 discusses this recent development in greater detail.

5 *Telephone counselling and information services*
Some areas have a local telephone counselling service which may offer advice about drugs as one of its functions. A telephone support service for people in a crisis is offered by the Samaritans. Other organisations will offer written material. This may come as specialist advice from groups like Alcohol Concern or be part of a general programme. For example, the Mothers' Union covers all sorts of personal problems in an excellent set of personal testimonies entitled *I was there*.

Conclusion

Despite the wide range of services available there is insufficient provision in Britain to meet the needs of everyone who has a drug problem. In obtaining services for addicts the important factor is actually to know where to go to get information. The practical section at the back of the book (Appendices 1 and 2) should help anyone wanting to do this.

11

The challenge of today

The day I wrote this last chapter I had spent the morning in a comprehensive school talking to a fourth form group about alcohol and other drugs. This was part of a term's programme (one hour per week) on the issue. I was attempting to demonstrate that the drug issue is part of life as a whole and that it was important for everyone to consider both their own personal health and their example to other people.

I divided the students into small groups and asked them to put a list of fifteen substances into priority order. The young people had to choose their own reasons for deciding which were the most and which were the least dangerous substances. The full list was: heroin; cannabis; chocolate; wine; LSD; tobacco; benzodiazepines; barbiturates; amphetamines; coffee; glue; caffeine; cocaine; magic mushrooms; alcohol.

Heroin stood out as the drug which the students considered to be the most dangerous – despite the fact that less than one in every hundred teenagers have ever tried it. Cocaine was listed as the next important. This is a drug which has received a lot of publicity and (at this time) was used by even fewer people. LSD came third – probably because it sounded dangerous and the Acid House culture was just beginning. Alcohol came fourth despite the fact that, as we have seen, it affects millions more people than the illegal drugs and costs us millions of pounds each year in road accident and health service costs, etc. The young people perceived heroin, cocaine and LSD to be the most dangerous drugs because they were illegal and had a high profile at the time. Tobacco was completely unplaced, as were solvents – and yet these are substances which many young people use every day.

It is because they share mis-perceptions like these that Christians may feel today's drug scene to be an irrelevance. Nobody actually says this, but the inaction shown by many demonstrates it to be true. If we believe that the most dangerous drugs are those which are used by a small minority of people then we will also believe that they do not affect us personally. If we believe that alcohol and tobacco are not dangerous then we will not see the harm that these drugs can – and do – cause.

The fact of the matter is that many people are at risk from legal, as well as illegal, drugs. They need help long before a crisis occurs. The challenge is for Christians to get there well before this stage. We have Jesus to offer to everybody. An increase in Christian social action coupled with a desire to offer people the gospel would bring a reduction in drug-related problems. It happened in the nineteenth century and it can happen today. Today's drug scene is a challenge – or rather it offers a variety of challenges.

It is a challenge to Christianity because our society's dependence on drugs offers something else that will take the place of a living faith. A lifestyle dependent on one or more drugs will leave little room for one which is able to accept what God has to offer.

It is a challenge because Jesus told us to love our neighbours. Whether we care for people by helping to solve existing problems or by a positive example which helps avoid those problems in the first place we are doing God's work. There are so many ways to do this that nobody can disclaim responsibility for doing something, no matter how little they know about the drink and drug scene. Everyone can pray. Everyone can have a personal, positive example. Love, caring, sharing and encouragement are all relevant words in living out the Christian gospel.

It is a challenge to cut through all the misinformation and mythology that surrounds the drug world: to understand what is going on and to show others the reality of life. And ill-informed ideas matter because they lead to the wrong action. If we believe that anyone who takes a drug is in imminent danger of overdose then panic may be the first response to a drug user rather than a more careful appraisal of the situation. If we think drug addicts are all young layabouts then we fail to understand the need for support of, for example, the many, many people who look to tranquillisers to see them through the day. Nobody needs to be an expert on drugs, although it does help to have a certain basic knowledge.

It is a challenge that is personal. It is impossible to get away from the question of example. Using the 'Christian lifestyle' principles which were identified in the fourth chapter, see what you think about what this twenty-two year old has written.

At home I'd been used to the odd glass of wine at meals or for celebrations, but never in excess or regularly. However, at university I saw nothing wrong in becoming a 'normal' student – which involved going to the bar every night for a social drink. Even then I didn't drink much – a half or a full pint of cider – but, as my friends said, in my case it didn't take much!

Then I found my faith in Christ and suddenly I no longer needed to go to the pub to enjoy myself. I had great fun with my friends over a cup of coffee, playing sport or going for walks.

Although my pub visits stopped, I still had wine with meals and it wasn't until I began to see the effect of alcohol on those around me that I started to think about my drinking. This, coupled with the knowledge that my example had persuaded someone else to start drinking and that my body was described in the Bible as the temple of the Holy Spirit, helped me stop completely.

I am not a 'recovered alcoholic' and I think that I am fairly normal. I still know that I do not need alcohol or any other social drug to live my life. I have been drug-free for well over two years now and can truly say that I have had a much better time than when I was socially drinking.

I do understand how drink is so much part of the way of life in this country, but I also know that my Christian witness is none the worse for my total abstinence and I am convinced that there are situations where it has been positively improved.

As we have seen, the Bible does not give any firm advice as to whether Christians should be total abstainers or 'responsible drinkers', although it does come out strongly against drunkenness. It leaves us with the responsibility to make up our own minds.

Alcohol and other drugs will always pose questions for Christians. Some of them will not be easy to answer, but if we are going to be an example for Christ then they cannot be ignored. Perhaps the best starting point for any of us is to ask the question, 'What would Jesus do if he was here in my situation?'

Appendix 1

Local services

One of the best sources of information is the local Citizens Advice Bureau. Advice can also be sought from the local Health Authorities, Social Services Department, Youth Service and local Council on Alcoholism or Drugs Information Centre. Of course, some areas have Christian projects and/or workers who can be approached for advice. Local Christian youth workers or ministers could be asked to see if they have come across any specifically Christian workers.

Appendix 2

Useful addresses

An asterisk indicates that the agency listed is specifically Christian.

Education and information

Information can be obtained from a number of agencies. Local NHS Health Promotion Departments will have leaflets, as will any drug information centre or Council on Alcoholism. Nationally, secular bodies like the Institute for the Study of Drugs Dependence, Alcohol Concern and The Advisory Council on Alcohol and Drug Education (TACADE) all provide useful material.

There is also the material and other services produced by Christian organisations such as the UK Band of Hope. Most of the denominations will have produced some source material (or be able to recommend someone else's).

Youth organisations like British Youth For Christ have produced leaflets and there will be sections on alcohol and drug abuse in many youth handbooks. The Band of Hope produces an attractive range of literature and services particularly aimed at children and young people and offers a free resource catalogue.

The United Kingdom Temperance Alliance has founded the Institute of Alcohol Studies and the 'Stay Dry' Campaign, both of which provide useful information for adults and older students respectively.

A number of organisations, including the Christian rehabilitation houses, are willing to supply speakers.

***UK Band of Hope**, 25(F) Copperfield Street, London SE1 0EN (Tel: 071–928 0848)

***Evangelical Coalition on Drugs**, Evangelical Alliance, Whitefield House, 186 Kennington Park Road, London SE11 4BT (Tel: 071–582 0228)

Alcohol Concern, 305 Gray's Inn Road, London WC1X 8QF (Tel: 071–833 3471)

***The Mothers' Union**, Social Affairs Department, The Mary Sumner House, 24 Tufton Street, London SW1P 3RB (Tel: 071–222 5533)

ReSolv, The Society for the Prevention of Solvent and Volatile Substance Abuse, St Mary's Chambers, 19 Station Road, Stone, Staffordshire ST15 8JP (Tel: 0785 817885)

Institute for the Study of Drugs Dependence, 1 Hatton Garden, London EC1N 8ND (Tel: 071–430 1991)

TACADE, 1 Hulme Place, The Crescent, Salford, Manchester M5 4QA (Tel: 061–745 8925)

UK Temperance Alliance (includes Institute of Alcohol Studies and 'Stay Dry' Campaign), Alliance House, 12 Caxton Street, London SW1 (Tel: 071–222 5880)

Rehabilitation, counselling and self-help groups

Al-Anon, 61 Great Dover Street, London SE1 4YF (Tel: 071–403 0888)

Alcohol Concern, 305 Gray's Inn Road, London WC1X 8QF (Tel: 071–833 3471) (They have a directory of alcohol services throughout Britain.)

Alcoholics Anonymous, PO Box 1, Stonebow House, Stonebow, York YO1 2NJ (Tel: 0904 644026)

*__Coke Hole Trust__, 70 Junction Road, Andover, Hampshire SP10 3QX (Tel: 0264 61745)

Institute for the Study of Drugs Dependence, 1 Hatton Garden, London EC1N 8ND (Tel: 071–430 1991) (They have a national directory of services for drug abusers.)

*__Kaleidoscope Trust__, 40–46 Cromwell Road, Kingston-upon-Thames, Surrey (Tel: 081–549 2681/7488)

*__Kenward Trust__, Kenward House, Yalding, Kent ME18 6AH (Tel: 0622 812603)

The Life-Anew Trust, Clouds House, East Knoyle, Salisbury, Wiltshire SP3 6BE (Tel: 074378 3733)

MIND (National Association for Mental Health), 22 Harley Street, London W1 (Tel: 071–637 0741)

ReSolv, The Society for the Prevention of Solvent and Volatile Substance Abuse, St Mary's Chambers, 19 Station Road, Stone, Staffordshire ST15 8JP (Tel: 0785 817885)

*Stauros Foundation, 54b Shelling Hill Road, Cullybackey, Ballymena, N. Ireland (Tel: 0266 886374)

Turning Point, CAP House, 9–12 Long Lane, London EC1A 9HA (Tel: 071–606 3947/9)

***UK Band of Hope**, 25 (F) Copperfield Street, London SE1 0EN (Tel: 071–928 0848) (For a directory of Christian based services.)

***Yeldall Manor**, Blakes Lane, Hare Hatch, Twyford, Reading, Berkshire RG10 9XR (Tel: 0734 404411)

Advertising complaints

The Advertising Standards Authority, Brook House, 2–16 Torrington Place, London WC1E 7HN (Tel: 071–580 5555)

The Independent Broadcasting Authority and **The Advertising Advisory Committee,** 70 Brompton Road, London SW3 1EY (Tel: 071–584 7011)

Appendix 3

Emergency action on solvent abuse

When you find a sniffer semi-conscious or unconscious:

1 Remove the solvent.
2 Check that the mouth is clear and nothing is blocking the throat.
3 Lie the person down on his or her stomach with the head to one side to prevent vomit from being inhaled. Make sure there is no vomit in his or her mouth and do not leave them.

4 Get somebody to telephone 999 for an ambulance.

If the user is 'high' (intoxicated, ie staggering or generally out of control):

1 Remove the solvent whilst being firm and caring. Avoid an argument.
2 Loosen tight clothing, especially around the neck.
3 Ensure plenty of fresh air.
4 Give nothing to eat or drink.
5 Someone must stay with the user until he or she is fully conscious (recovery could take anything from fifteen minutes to a few hours).
6 Tell somebody (eg a parent or teacher) what has happened.

Look out for signs of sniffing:

1 Groups of young people acting strangely and behaving as if drunk.
2 Breath and clothing smelling of solvent.
3 Signs of glue, spots or sores around the nose and mouth; also solvent on clothing.
4 Empty crisp packets or solvent containers left in such places as waste ground, derelict buildings or even under beds.
5 A change in behaviour such as increased aggression, truancy or lack of concentration, slurred speech or unco-ordinated movements.

Help may be obtained from:

1 The family doctor.
2 Teachers.
3 The school health service.
4 Samaritans (for counselling facilities in the area).
5 ReSolv, The Society for the Prevention of Solvent and Volatile Substance Abuse, St Mary's Chambers, 19 Station Road, Stone, Staffordshire ST15 8JP (Tel: 0785 817885)

Note: It is best to find a doctor, teacher or counsellor

with experience in working with people who have solvent or other drug problems.

Appendix 4

Alcohol-free drinks

There is a wide range of attractive grape and other fruit juices available, with more coming on the market all the time. Other drinks have the taste and style of alcoholic drinks but do not contain alcohol. You have probably heard of alcohol-free lagers, but there are also wines with the alcohol removed, vermouths, bitters (like campari), pastis (like Pernod) and spirit flavoured drinks, including whisky and gin flavours. These are either made from the same ingredients as alcoholic drinks or are water-based with flavouring added. Alternative drinks are good for people who enjoy the taste, but not the effect, of alcohol and for those who are sensitive to being seen with a 'soft drink' yet wish to keep a clear head for driving, etc.

The brewers are producing more 'low-alcohol' lagers and beers (with less than 1% alcohol by volume). Some of these have less alcohol in them than fruit juices, which will all have a small amount which naturally occurs.

These drinks can usually be found in health food shops, food halls in department stores, delicatessens, some off-licences, supermarkets and pubs.

Alcoholic drinks require a licence for their sale and duty is paid on them. Unfortunately, in Britain there is no general name for the types of drinks which can be sold without a licence. Although some, of course, are soft drinks, this name is not really appropriate for all of them. Non-alcoholic is commonly used, but they may also be labelled 'alcohol-free' or 'low-alcohol'. Check the label, though, as some 'low alcohol' products still contain a significant amount of the drug.

Amethyst Refreshments of Reading have produced a useful booklet about alcohol-free drinks.

Sample recipes

Try a **Shirley Temple**! Take 2 parts pineapple juice; 1 part passion fruit nectar; 3 parts lemonade. Blend pineapple and passion fruit with ice. Pour into a small goblet and add lemonade. Garnish with a slice of pineapple and a cherry. Serve with two straws.

Or how about a **Brahms and auber**? Take: half a goblet of orange juice; quarter of a goblet of single cream; 1 banana. Blend till frothy and serve in a large goblet. Garnish with a slice of orange wrapped around a cherry on a cocktail stick. (The name *auber* comes from rhyming slang for 'sober'.)

Watch out for quarrels if you run out of **Meribah!** Take: half a glass of orange juice; half a glass of pineapple juice; a dash of grenadine syrup. Half fill the glass with crushed ice and then pour in the orange juice, add the pineapple and finally pour in the grenadine. This should sink to the bottom – give a quick stir to start it mixing but don't stir it in completely. Use two bendy straws and garnish with a parasol and pineapple on a cocktail stick.

Simpler drinks are **Diesel** (Cola with a dash of blackcurrant) or **St Clements** (a mixture of orange juice and lemonade).

Celebrations

Amethyst Refreshments Ltd stock a variety of sparkling dry and sweet grape juices and de-alcoholised wines that will make you wonder why you ever needed champagne!

Supermarkets and other shops stock brands such as Eisberg, Paul Masson Light and the old favourite, Schloer.

Remember that we all have different tastes and just as there are many different wines, so alcohol-free drinks are different and each of us will like some better than others.

Mail order

Amethyst Refreshments Ltd, 207 London Road, Reading, Berks RG1 3NT (Tel: 0734 663339) supply alcohol-free drinks on mail order.

Appendix 5

Discussion starters and activities

Discussion starters

1 What effects of (whichever drugs you like to discuss) have you seen around you at school or in the youth group?

2 Do you think people need to take illegal drugs when tobacco and alcohol are so readily available?

3 Can sniffing solvents lead to other drug problems?

4 'We can influence other people's lives by our example.' Discuss this.

5 What would Jesus have done about drink and other drugs if he was physically present today?

Activities

1 Cut out any articles on any aspect of drugs from newspapers (including references to alcohol and tobacco) and compare the different amounts of publicity given to the different drugs.
2 Act out various situations in which someone finds a person under the influence of a drug and the different responses which may be made.
3 Carry out a survey of young people to find out what they think about drug use.
4 Ask a school nurse, health visitor, policeman or youth worker to talk about one or more drugs. (Choose someone who has had actual experience of working with people who use drugs.)
5 Draw a poster encouraging people not to start taking any drugs. Give specific reasons rather than just saying No.
6 Have a non-alcoholic cocktails night with people mixing their own and experimenting.

Appendix 6

Recommended reading

Some of the books and leaflets used in the preparation of this book were:

Alcohol: Our Favourite Drug, Royal College of Psychiatrists
Through a Glass Darkly, Methodist Church Division of Social Responsibility
Guide to Opposing Liquor Licensing Applications, Methodist Church Division of Social Responsibility
A Lot Of Bottle, UK Temperance Alliance

Problem Drinking, Trades Union Congress
Drugs: What Every Parent Should Know, Institute for the Study of Drugs Dependence
Life in the Fast Lane (amphetamines and cocaine), UK Band of Hope
The New Booze Book, UK Band of Hope
Thinking of Drinking, UK Band of Hope
Trend (series on alcohol and other drugs), UK Band of Hope
Sniffing It Snuffing It, UK Band of Hope
Clearway (Alcohol and other drugs education programme), UK Band of Hope

Leaflets and other information are also produced by the organisations listed in Appendix 2.

Appendix 7

Harm reduction

(Adapted from a Drug Focus paper prepared by the Revd Charles Rutter, Churches and Information Co-ordinator of the UK Band of Hope.)

What is harm reduction? Sometimes called harm minimisation, it is a strategy for dealing with and trying to limit the harmful consequences of prohibited drug use, especially amongst intravenous drug users.

Harm reduction strategy is being developed in four areas: treatment, care, control and education.

Treatment and care

The following account by Eric Blakebrough describes how and why one Christian community has used the harm reduction model as their means of expressing the love of Christ.

'**Threefold Disability** Those individuals who have a variety of reasons for becoming dependent upon alcohol and other drugs are in a particularly bad condition. In addition to the problems which perhaps initiated their dependency, using drugs to avoid facing up to problems tends to retard emotional development. In the case of such drug dependents there is, therefore, a threefold disability:

1 The problems leading to dependency.
2 The physical and psychological dependency on the drug.
3 Retarded emotional development.

'It follows from this that we should not expect instant cures of drug dependents to be the general rule. It is desirable to provide some means of relieving pain and of treating the symptoms until such time as the root cause of the problem is dealt with. There are other cases where a condition seems to be incurable, pain relief and treating the symptoms being the only help we can offer.

'**Intervention and acceptance** At the Kaleidoscope Project in Kingston-upon-Thames, we have had extensive experience of harm minimisation as a means of assisting people with drug problems. One hundred and fifty heroin dependents now come daily for a dose of methadone which is administered orally in the presence of staff. This by itself is not a cure and is judged by some to reduce a person's will to be cured. If, however, this medical intervention is complemented by an experience of acceptance and the gradual building up of trustful relationships, this treatment can prove beneficial in the following ways:

1 Obtaining a legal prescription reduces the pressure towards criminal activity involved in obtaining an illicit supply of drugs.
2 The slow-acting properties of methadone enable a person to function without violent mood swings.

'Before AIDS was recognised, people working with drug dependents were encouraged by the fact that approximately one-third of people with a drug habit would overcome dependency in time. In such circumstances it might have been reasonable to advocate abstinence as the only goal of treatment. There was in a sense no hurry; a person could be allowed to sink to their lowest point in the expectation that eventually they would realise their desperate condition and find the necessary motivation to undergo treatment. This was perhaps never a very enlightened viewpoint but it made a good deal of sense.

'Such an approach is unthinkable today. A young person experimenting with drugs and sex is at risk of AIDS unless precautions are taken. In the circumstances it would indeed be a stern law-giver who would forbid any assistance to those at risk of dying. Harm minimisation in the form of condoms, clean needles and syringes, methadone and daily social support are the only responsible Christian reactions.

'It may be asked if this approach misses out the grace of God in Christ. Perhaps on reflection it can be seen that Christ is present in those who patiently offer treatment and that it is this non-judgmental acceptance of people which is the most effective proclamation of the Gospel in these cases.'

Control

Both deterrent and punitive mechanisms are employed by Government in an attempt to control illegal drug use. These include:

- International co-operation against those who produce and transport drugs.
- Confiscation of assets, heavy fines and imprisonment for convicted drug traffickers.

More controversially, the European Movement for the Normalisation of Drug Policy opposes what they see as the destructive effects of prohibition on society and aims to create a 'humane drug policy' by making possession of drugs a non-criminal offence.

The official attitude

The Advisory Council on the Misuse of Drugs published a report which stated: 'The spread of HIV is a greater danger to individual and public health than drug misuse. Accordingly, we believe that services which aim to minimize HIV risk behaviour by all available means should take precedence in development plans.'

The main concern is that HIV infection should not spread. The use of dirty needles and poor injecting techniques is a principal cause in the spread of HIV, hence the efforts to provide clean equipment.

The official endorsement of harm reduction strategy is a response to the public health hazard of spreading HIV/AIDS infection. Drug use is seen as the lesser evil. Since the advent of AIDS, is it unreasonable (as Eric Blakebrough suggests) to advocate abstinence? AIDS is spread in a variety of ways (sexual activity, needle sharing, blood transfusion) and the main danger of HIV, with regard to needle sharing, is in the context of promiscuous behaviour. The biblical emphasis is upon chastity before marriage and faithfulness within marriage. Often, needle sharing and sexual activity go together. It is argued by some that such activity is regulated more effectively by the use of methadone.

Education

The Department of Health Report *AIDS and Drug Misuse* points out that prevention of drug misuse is now more important than ever before.

The 'sensible use' approach A leaflet put out by one druglink agency carries the heading 'Are you injecting drugs?' Inside, it describes a safer way to inject: 'It is better not to inject, but if you do, sharing works (needle and syringe) means sharing sickness (such as Hepatitis and AIDS) so never share works, even with your best friend. Contact us to find out about getting clean needles and syringes' (there then follows advice on how to clean works if 'as a last resort, you do share'). There is information on the disposal of used needles and the importance of using condoms for safer sex. Also included is advice on healthy diet and sleep.

For injecting drug users, this approach offers a form of harm reduction which opens up the possibility of ongoing contact and counselling through a helping agency.

Comment

Harm reduction is not an easy answer to drug problems; indeed it raises a number of difficult questions. The first, and most obvious is: 'Does it work?' It is arguable that the experience of countries with a longer history of harm reduction as a strategy shows that thousands of young heroin addicts spend years becoming middle-aged methadone addicts! Harm reduction is also a difficult strategy to employ, in that drawing the line between people who will be helped by a harm reduction strategy and those who will be helped by a 'Just say No' approach is not easy. Harm reduction has critics who deserve to be heard. It is a philosophy which does not sit easily with many of the principles outlined in this book.

One issue which must be given prominence when considering harm reduction is that it logically should only apply to established drug abusers – and even then only when any alternative policy seems likely to fail. With those who are on the fringes of drug abuse, who use legal drugs in moderation or who do not use drugs at all, the emphasis must be on harm avoidance – ie a positive encouragement to drug-free living.

We have a real problem when harm reduction is applied to prevention as this runs directly against many of the biblical lifestyle principles outlined earlier in this book.

Conclusion

While harm avoidance should be the main emphasis in the churches' teaching, the dilemmas of dealing with alcohol and other drug-related problems remain. Harm reduction in some form is essential as a compassionate response to such people.

The issues as they relate to good pastoral practice may be summarised as follows:

- People with drug dependency problems must be cared for and helped.
- If some form of harm minimisation is appropriate for users, how should this be practised in conjunction with the needs of non-users?
- What effect would harm reduction strategies have upon a local church community?
- The dilemmas posed by harm reduction make the need for effective harm avoidance through preventative education an absolute imperative.
- Whatever policy is adopted, working relationships need to be established with local doctors and drug agencies.
- Christian ministry is rooted in the power of God to change lives. It is not expressed in judgment, or laying down the law, but in showing and sharing the love of

Jesus with people for whom God wants nothing but the best.

Whether or not you agree with harm reduction, these issues need careful and prayerful consideration.